Development of FDA-Regulated Medical Products

Prescription Drugs, Biologics, and Medical Devices

Also available from ASQ Quality Press:

The FDA and Worldwide Quality System Requirements Guidebook for Medical Devices
Kimberly A.Trautman

The Quality Auditor's HACCP Handbook
ASQ Food, Drug, and Cosmetic Division

Mastering and Managing the FDA Maze
Gordon Harnack

Product Recall Planning Guide, Second Edition
ASQ Product Safety and Liability Prevention Interest Group

To request a complimentary catalog of ASQ Quality Press publications, call (800) 248-1946, or visit our bookstore at http://www.asq.org.

Development of FDA-Regulated Medical Products

Prescription Drugs, Biologics, and Medical Devices

Elaine Whitmore

ASQ Quality Press
Milwaukee, Wisconsin

American Society for Quality, Quality Press, Milwaukee 53203
© 2004 by ASQ
All rights reserved. Published 2003
Printed in the United States of America

12 11 10   5 4 3

Library of Congress Cataloging-in-Publication Data

Whitmore, Elaine.
  Development of FDA-regulated medical products : prescription drugs,
biologics, and medical devices / Elaine Whitmore.—2nd ed.
    p. cm.
  Previously published under the title: Product development planning for
health care products regulated by the FDA.
  Includes bibliographical references and index.
  ISBN 0-87389-613-0 (hardcover, case bound)
    1. Drug approval—United States. 2. New products—Standards—United
States. 3. United States. Food and Drug Administration. I. Whitmore,
Elaine. Product development planning for health care products regulated
by the FDA. II. Title.

RA401.5.W48 2003
615'.19—dc22   2003023464

Publisher: William A. Tony
Acquisitions Editor: Annemieke Hytinen
Project Editor: Paul O'Mara
Production Administrator: Randy Benson
Special Marketing Representative: Robin Barry

ASQ Mission: The American Society for Quality advances individual,
organizational, and community excellence worldwide through learning,
quality improvement, and knowledge exchange.

Attention Bookstores, Wholesalers, Schools, and Corporations: ASQ Quality
Press books, videotapes, audiotapes, and software are available at quantity
discounts with bulk purchases for business, educational, or instructional use.
For information, please contact ASQ Quality Press at 800-248-1946, or write to
ASQ Quality Press, P.O. Box 3005, Milwaukee, WI 53201-3005.

To place orders or to request a free copy of the ASQ Quality Press Publications
Catalog, including ASQ membership information, call 800-248-1946. Visit our
Web site at www.asq.org or http://qualitypress.asq.org.

 Printed on acid-free paper

Quality Press
600 N. Plankinton Avenue
Milwaukee, Wisconsin 53203
Call toll free 800-248-1946
Fax 414-272-1734
www.asq.org
http://qualitypress.asq.org
http://standardsgroup.asq.org
E-mail: authors@asq.org

For Don, Andy, and Laura—as always.

Table of Contents

List of Figures and Tables

Foreword

Healthcare cost, quality and access, and the question of "Who pays?" have taken center stage in the United States. By focusing on the political, economic, and societal influences on medical product development in updating her 1997 book, Elaine Whitmore directs us to the critical wave of change that has rolled across the pharmaceutical industry. The drug development industry has experienced sometimes gut-wrenching transformation in the past decade and, as far as anyone can tell, this transformation will continue to evolve as strong outside influences on product development continue to exert tremendous pressures.

Will the latest push to cut the cost of prescription drugs, biotechnology, or new medical technology result in dampening innovation in the regulated industries? We all hope it won't, but the truth is we don't know. This volume helps put focus on the various issues that impact this concern:

- When will the regulatory environment change again?

- How has the focus on patient outcomes affected product development?

- How will increased social pressures to manage medical costs affect marketing objectives and the product lifecycle?

- Will the United States adopt European pricing practices? How might this impact product development and patient care?

As a business leader in the pharmaceutical industry whose career has been intimately tied to the product development process, I find *Development of FDA-Regulated Medical Products* to be comprehensive, inclusive and well organized. The first step in mastering this changing environment is to better understand it.

For those who have made a career in pharmaceuticals, or are involved in the product development cycle, Elaine's text is suitable as a helpful day-to-day guide. It offers insight as to how internal and external pressures influence the modern medical product development process, and how these pressures interact with one another. With this knowledge, medical product development professionals will be better able to synthesize the elements of the new development process, and achieve the ultimate objective of bringing an effective product to market.

Elaine's text also gives us an excellent basis from which to begin an analysis of product development decision making. And it is my hope that others outside the industry, especially those who are striving to better understand how we work, will leave with a better understanding of why and how product decisions are made, and the very significant level of risk and challenge inherent in the process.

In my mind, the real insight that Elaine Whitmore can offer us comes through in her very last chapter entitled, "Where Do We Go from Here?" In it, she talks about a great many practical issues that revolve around managing expectations at all levels of the company, managing interactions between members of the development team, and the key role of technology in the development process.

But the real issue remains: "Where do we go from here?" Dr. Whitmore acknowledges that the medical product development landscape is constantly evolving, and provides stimulus for future discussion and debate that should occur across our industry.

With the tremendous challenges, risks, and external pressures of developing new medicines and devices in the 21st century, it is still a wonder that new products are developed at all. That said, it would be a tragedy if they were not. And that is the very reason why Elaine Whitmore's work is so critical.

Carrie S. Cox
President, Global Pharmaceuticals
Schering-Plough
Kenilworth, New Jersey

Preface

Since the predecessor to this book on product development was published in 1997, under the rather unwieldy title *Product Development Planning for Healthcare Products Regulated by the FDA,* there have been revolutionary changes to the classification and regulation of prescription drugs, biologics, and medical devices. One effect of the modernization of the Food and Drug Administration (FDA) has been a leveling of the playing field in the 21st century, with both regulators and industry experiencing the uncertainties and growing pains that accompany significant government reorganization.

While focus and missions in medical product development will always be functions, to some extent, of political and social change, certain principles remain intact: there is a need for new medical products that are safe and effective, designed and developed with quality, and that meet the needs of customers. Efficiently and productively fulfilling these objectives requires effective coordination of product development processes and activities.

Much new information has been added, including a review of the significant changes within the FDA that affect the requirements and review of medical products; updated facts and figures; expansion of subjects that have grown more critical, such as clinical outcomes, human factors, and marketing objectives; and new topics, such as the role of product development in hazard analysis, recalls, and product liability. The basic philosophical message of the earlier volume and the intended audience of anyone interested in or active in medical product development—regardless of corporate function—remain the same.

Preface to Previous Edition*

This book is about maximizing the efficiency of developing new healthcare products—such as medical devices, biologics, and drugs—that are regulated by the FDA. This book is not intended to emphasize that product development is important, that businesses need new products to survive and to grow, or that the results of poorly executed product development are costly or disastrous. Anyone interested in product development already knows this.

After several years of searching for a volume or two that would offer information helpful to my product development endeavors in this field, I discovered that conventional product development literature simply does not address topics of significance to healthcare products. Why is the development of medical devices, drugs, and biologics unique enough to warrant a dedicated, up-to-date examination? There are many reasons, not the least of which involves regulations. The requirements of the FDA, coupled with those of emerging international regulatory and quality standards, differentiate healthcare products from the products that are the subjects of most product development literature. Testing programs required by regulatory agencies before healthcare products can be marketed impose special constraints on development time lines, as do the often lengthy regulatory review processes. Managed care, as well, is exerting a profound influence, by requiring demonstration of superior clinical, cost, and quality-of-life outcomes. Other factors such as cultural differences in attitudes, practices, and preferred outcomes of medicine and surgery pose special challenges to globalizing product development efforts and new product introductions.

Organizational challenges exist, too. Product development must go on through restructuring, reorganization, mergers, divestitures, and the sequential adoption of the latest trends in organizational philosophy. The way a particular company is structured or managed may or may not be

---

* Whitmore, Elaine. *Product Development Planning for Health Care Products Regulated by the FDA*. Milwaukee: ASQ Quality Press, 1997.

optimal for product development in that company at a given time. Generally speaking, though, those individuals actively involved in product development do not have the authority to make substantial changes in organizational structure. Consequently, it is important for healthcare product development guidelines to be applicable to most, if not all, corporate structures, and not to require force-fitting.

This book is intended to form a foundation for anyone—regardless of functional specialty or organizational echelon—who is a student of, is about to embark upon, is active in, or has management responsibility for product development and business development decisions in the medical device and pharmaceuticals industry. This book is also appropriate for upper management personmel not personally active in product development activities, because it raises and explains issues pertinent to the success of healthcare product development efforts. Although not arranged in textbook format, the material is well-suited for classroom use in advanced management or specialty management programs.

This is not a how-to manual, for the scope of FDA-regulated healthcare products is too vast to address in any single volume using a step-by-step approach. Rather than teaching readers how to do things, this book instructs readers about the nature of the things that need to be done for the successful development and commercialization of new healthcare products. There are requirements that apply to product development of FDA-regulated healthcare products that are never encountered or considered in the development of other categories of new products. After reading this book, individuals involved in the development of new FDA-regulated healthcare products, regardless of background or functional discipline, will understand the reasons and significance of these special requirements and appreciate the value of product development planning.

This book will provide readers with: (1) the basic background material that will allow cross-functional participants in product development, as well as managers not directly involved with the day-to-day activities of product development, to have a mutual understanding of regulations, guidelines, time lines, process implementation, and expectations; (2) a common vocabulary for all functions and all organizational levels; and (3) an introduction to methods and exercises that will facilitate quality-oriented healthcare product development. Through establishing a shared vision among diverse groups and individuals, product development planning can make healthcare product development activities less fractious and more productive.

Abbreviations

510(k)—premarket notification application

ANDA—abbreviated new drug application

BLA—biologics license application

CBA—cost/benefit analysis

CBER—Center for Biologics Evaluation and Research

CDER—Center for Drug Evaluation and Research

CDRH—Center for Devices and Radiological Health

CEA—cost-effectiveness analysis

cGMP—current good manufacturing practice

CMA—cost minimization analysis

CRO—contract research organization

CTD—common technical document

CUA—cost/utility analysis

FDA—Food and Drug Administration

FDAMA—Food and Drug Administration Modernization Act

FD&C Act—Food, Drug, and Cosmetic Act

FMEA—failure mode and effects analysis

FMECA—failure mode and effects criticality analysis

FTA—fault tree analysis

GCP—good clinical practice

GLP—good laboratory practice

GMP—good manufacturing practice

HFE—human factors engineering

ICH—International Conference on Harmonization (of technical requirements for registration of pharmaceuticals for human use)

IDE—investigational device exemption

IND—investigational new drug application

IP—intellectual property

IRB—Institutional Review Board

ISO—International Organization for Standardization

IVD—in vitro diagnostics

MDUFMA—Medical Device User Fee and Modernization Act

NCE—new chemical entity

NDA—new drug application

NME—new molecular entity

PDUFA—Prescription Drug User Fee Act

PHS Act—Public Health Service Act

PMA—premarket approval application

QOL—quality of life

QSR—quality systems regulations

SMDA—Safe Medical Devices Act

TQM—total quality management

Part I

Unique Challenges in Medical Product Development

1

Healthcare in the United States

The first wealth is health.

—Ralph Waldo Emerson

A billion here, a billion there, and pretty soon you're talking about real money.

—Everett Dirksen

Those involved in medical product development share the same primary goal: to discover, develop, and bring to market new products that enable people to live healthier, more productive, more comfortable lives. Nowhere in the world is this goal more enthusiastically endorsed by the population than in the United States. Yet from day one in the product development process, medical products manufacturers face challenges that other industries never have to confront.

The United States leads the world in healthcare spending.[1] Health and well-being are so important in this country that by 2001, annual national health expenditures represented 14.1 percent of the gross domestic product, or about $5000 per person. This means that in 2001, Americans spent more than $1.4 trillion on healthcare—more than five times the amount spent in 1980.[2] Government projections anticipate that this spending will exceed $3 trillion by 2012 (see Figure 1.1).

In recent years, spending on prescription drugs has grown at a faster rate than any other type of health expenditure. Prescription drug expenditures

Total U.S. Healthcare Spending

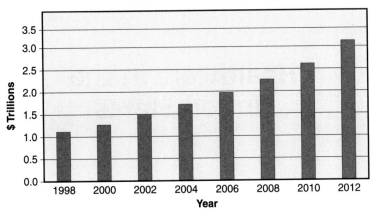

Figure 1.1   U.S. healthcare expenditures and projections.

Source: Centers for Medicare and Medicaid Services

U.S. Healthcare Spending—Prescription Drugs

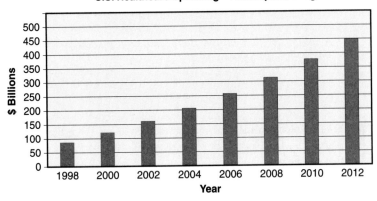

Figure 1.2   U.S. prescription drug expenditures and projections.

Source: Centers for Medicare and Medicaid Services

alone accounted for fully 10 percent of the money spent in the United States on healthcare in 2001. By 2012, spending on prescription drugs is expected to represent 15 percent of the total U.S. healthcare expenditure. As shown in Figure 1.2, the dollar amount spent on prescription drugs in 2012 will more than triple the 2001 prescription drug expenditure. Unlike prescription drug expenditures, spending on medical devices and biologics is not specifically tracked by the U.S. Department of Health and Human Services.

Industry estimates suggest that medical device sales in the United States were about $78 billion in 2000.[3] The biologics market may be about $40 billion and is rapidly rising.

Add up the numbers and it becomes clear that the market for prescription drugs and other healthcare products, including medical devices and biological products, is staggeringly huge. Continued growth and profitability, however, depend on a delicate balance of managed care initiatives, federal and international regulatory requirements, generic challenges, liability issues, and the ability of industry suppliers and manufacturers to shorten product development cycles.

Product development in the healthcare field, especially product development of medical devices and certain biologics, has all too often been a seat-of-the-pants endeavor, short-changed in terms of support and understanding by management and by the individuals charged with getting the job done. But with recent developments in healthcare management and with sweeping changes in global clinical, regulatory, and quality requirements, manufacturers will no longer be able to effectively compete in the arena of healthcare products without making equally sweeping changes in the way they develop new products. The Food and Drug Administration (FDA) has taken on a new role in enabling these changes, as will be discussed in chapter 2.

Manufacturers of medical products today are obligated to do more than simply provide evidence to the FDA that their products are safe and efficacious. Growing concerns about the cost and quality of healthcare in the United States will dictate that in order for a new product to be accepted, reimbursed, and perhaps even approved, the use of that product will have to provide favorable outcomes in terms of:

- Clinical utility in uncontrolled real-life use situations

- Quality of life for the patient, following the treatment

- Cost-effectiveness

Thus, a successful product development process will need to factor in therapeutic, humanistic, and economic performance.

It takes a lot of money and time to develop and launch a medical product. It is estimated that in the United States, about 10 to 15 years and more than $800 million are needed to develop and obtain approval for a new drug.[4] Investments in the development of new therapeutic biologics are similar. Because the medical device area is much more diverse and complex, it is difficult to come up with average development times. Average time from concept to commercialization for medical devices ranges from two years to seven years, depending on the type of regulatory application required.[5]

Regulatory requirements and quality standards are becoming more demanding, in part because of the desire to market new products outside of the United States. The shrinking of the world through globalization of medical product businesses is a fact of life for a variety of reasons: (1) the domestic market is becoming increasingly saturated, so that going global is one of the few remaining ways to grow; (2) the pressures of managed care and cost containment in the United States are making it more difficult to increase domestic sales of products that do not have demonstrated outcomes advantages when compared with available lower-priced alternatives; (3) small companies partner with or get acquired by large companies, the overwhelming majority of which have a multinational presence; and (4) large, multinational companies want products that they can market globally. Yet many healthcare companies are poorly prepared to integrate into their product development plans the elements of cultural biases and preferences in medical and surgical practices, differing expectations of acceptable clinical outcomes, and variability in regulatory and quality requirements.

Harmonization of domestic requirements, as defined by the FDA, with those set forth by the International Conference on Harmonization (ICH) directives will be a process requiring ongoing evolution and refinement. One thing is certain: harmonization will directly affect the way product development is planned, executed, and documented.

Because of the enormous investments required for regulated medical product development, a shotgun approach often used with nonmedical product categories—in which large numbers of new products are introduced in hopes of ending up with at least one big winner—is not possible. Extraordinary focus and foresight are necessary. Evaluation of a myriad of ideas and opportunities against well-defined criteria will help assure that resources are directed at a select few of those opportunities—those that will lead to successful and profitable new products.

Even though the pharmaceutical/medical device industry spends proportionately more on research and development (R&D), as a percent of sales, than other industries, much of that money ends up being misdirected into activities that do not yield either information that is useful or new products that are profitable. Industrial R&D intensity and expenditure do not guarantee success. The R&D efforts must be coupled to product and process developments that will sustain the company through the present and into the future. It is not uncommon for 50 percent or more of what is called R&D or product development activity to be delegated to work related to neither research nor development. Requests for technical fixes for existing products with design flaws usually top the list. Responding to field sales forces when help is needed with customer questions or problems, and revalidating processes and products after the company makes changes in materials, equipment, or manufacturing location, are also typical. Add to this the time spent on general administrative tasks, various updates and pre-sentations, and training programs, and it's clear that not much time may be left for developing new products or technologies.

For a healthcare company to attain or sustain leadership will require the timely development and launch of new products that are safe and effective, meet both recognized and unarticulated user needs, and provide necessary and desirable outcomes. Creating and using a system of *product develop-ment planning* will substantially increase the probability of achieving these goals. Product development planning should be thought of as the application of total quality management (TQM) principles to new medical products.

Product development planning is an integrative approach to addressing both long-term and short-term needs and requirements for new products (see Figure 1.3). Although each component section of product development planning will be discussed separately in this book, in practice the compo-nents are inseparable. Each component draws upon, as well as contributes to, every other component.

Product development planning defines a technology strategy by linking technology forecasting—as a vision of the future—with an ongoing assess-ment of existing, new, emerging, and embryonic technologies. The technol-ogy strategy, in turn, provides the foundation and direction for a portfolio of product development project opportunities. Finally, quality management of this development portfolio depends upon successful implementation of a sound product development process. The major components of product development process, development portfolio management, technology assessment, and technology forecasting overlap in their contributions to short-, medium-, and long-term strategy for the growth and evolution of the company (see Figure 1.4).

Firmly anchored in the present, the product development process deals with the immediacy of identified active projects; its impact on the future is dependent upon the development time line of each project. Portfolio man-agement assures the proper mix of product development projects and of their sequence and phasing; its impact is linked to the present and near-future through monitoring and management of active ongoing projects, and to the mid-term future through staged application of the product develop-ment process to other identified projects. Technology assessment spans the near- to mid-term future by encompassing evaluation of existing, emerging, embryonic, and new technology opportunities. Finally, the mid- to long-term future is most influenced by the imaginative, visionary exercise of technology forecasting.

Product development planning, especially through the implementation of the principles of the product development process, will allow healthcare

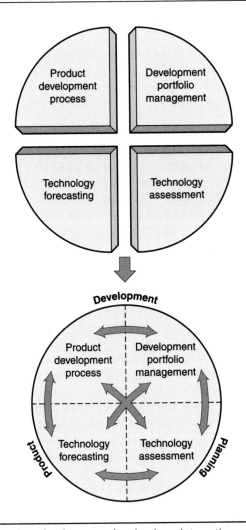

Figure 1.3   Product development planning is an integrative approach.

companies to break out of the trap of technical service disguising itself as R&D and undermining bona fide product development activities. Product design deficiencies and manufacturing problems will be identified and corrected early, making it much less likely for a costly problem to turn up late in the game. The lack of clarity or comfort in the handling and use of the product will be minimized or eliminated, reducing the demands for technical assurances, explanations, and support to users of the products. Furthermore,

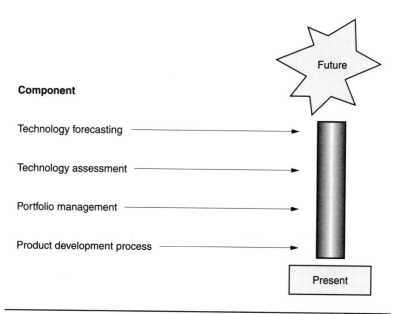

Figure 1.4   Product development planning.

a company will be less likely to suffer the embarrassment and cost of launching a product that is later discovered to have problems with properties such as usability, stability, or packaging. Most importantly, however, product-associated risks to patients will be reduced.

A few of the techniques and procedural suggestions that follow are especially tailored for the development of one or another category of medical product. For the most part, though, the principles and philosophy are also applicable to all categories of FDA-regulated medical products that are the focus of this book: drugs, biologics, and medical devices. A fundamental knowledge and understanding of all three categories of regulated medical products is unavoidably important, since new and more sophisticated technological approaches to meet customer needs have blurred the distinctions between drugs, biologics, and devices. While there may be differences in costs and development times, and in the nature and extent of regulatory and clinical requirements between the various categories of healthcare products, a program of formal and organized product development planning will bring focus and direction to everyone involved in medical product development and will add value and profitability to the products being developed.

2

It's Not Your Father's FDA

The "Modernization" of Medical Product Regulation

Regulations grow at the same rate as weeds.

—Norman R. Augustine

Hell hath no fury like a bureaucrat scorned.

—Milton Friedman

Drugs, biologics, and medical devices are among the $1 trillion worth of products regulated by the FDA. The FDA is charged with protecting American consumers by enforcing the Federal Food, Drug, and Cosmetic (FD&C) Act of 1938 (commonly referred to as "the Act") and a variety of other federal health laws (see Table 2.1). Over the years, critics of the FDA became increasingly convinced that the ability of the agency to accomplish its mission was not keeping pace with its obligations. In its effort to maintain the critical balance between the promotion of benefit and the prevention of harm, the FDA became bogged down in a quagmire of complex, unwieldy, and burdensome self-inflicted requirements.

A legislative reform effort to streamline FDA regulatory procedures, to improve the review of regulated products, and to increase and accelerate access to safe and effective medical products culminated with the creation of a modernization initiative. On November 21, 1997, the Food and Drug Administration Modernization Act (FDAMA) was enacted, amending some of the FD&C Act regulations applicable to drugs, biologics, and medical devices.[6] With the passage of FDAMA, Congress enhanced the FDA's mission

Table 2.1   Chronology of significant regulations relevant to healthcare product development.

Regulation	Purpose
1902 Biologies Control Act	Ensures purity and safety of serums, vaccines, and similar products used to prevent or treat diseases in humans
1906 Food and Drugs Act	Prohibits interstate commerce in misbranded and adulterated foods, drinks, and drugs
1938 Food, Drug, and Cosmetics Act	Requires new drugs to be shown safe before marketing, and extended control to therapeutic devices and cosmetics
1944 Public Health Service Act	Addresses broad spectrum of health concerns, including regulation of biological products for human use
1962 Kefauver-Harris Drug Amendments	Requires drug manufactures to prove to the FDA the effectiveness of their products and to obtain approval before marketing them
1966 Fair Packaging and Labeling Act	Requires consumer products, including drugs and medical devices, to be honestly and informatively labeled
1968 Radiation Control for Health and Safety Act	Protects public from unnecessary exposure to radiation from radiation-emitting products
1976 Medical Device Amendments	Ensures safety and effectiveness of medical devices, including diagnostic products, and requires manufacturers to register with the FDA
1983 Orphan Drug Act	Enables FDA to promote research and approval and marketing of drugs which would otherwise not be profitable but which are needed for treating rare diseases
1984 Drug Price Competition and Patent Term Restoration Act	Allows approval of generic versions of brand-name drugs without repeating safety and efficacy studies; allows brand-name companies to apply for up to five years' additional patent protection to compensate for time lost during FDA approval process
1990 Safe Medical Devices Act	Requires reporting of any medical device causing or contributing to the death, serious illness, or injury of a patient; requires manufacturers to conduct post-market surveillance of implanted devices
1992 Medical Device Amendments	Expands requirements for registration, certification, documentation, reporting, and surveillance of medical devices
1992 Prescription Drug User Fee Act	Requires drug and biologics manufacturers to pay fees to FDA for product applications and supplements

continued

continued

Regulation	Purpose
1997 Food and Drug Administration Modernization Act	Makes numerous changes to the rules governing FDA and regulated industries and enacts many FDA initiatives in the Reinventing Government program
2002 Medical Device Fee and Modernization Act	Allows FDA to collect fees to review medical device submissions

in ways that recognized that the agency needed the capacity to operate in a 21st century characterized by increasing technological, trade, and public health complexities.

FDAMA comprises major reforms to the way FDA regulates products under its jurisdiction. The following are the most important provisions of the act that apply to medical products.

PRESCRIPTION DRUG USER FEES

The act reauthorizes the Prescription Drug User Fee Act of 1992 (PDUFA). The user fees have allowed the FDA to add resources, reducing the review time for drugs and biologics.

FDA INITIATIVES AND PROGRAMS

FDAMA enacts many FDA initiatives undertaken in recent years under former Vice President Al Gore's Reinventing Government program. The codified initiatives include measures to:

- Modernize the regulation of biological products by bringing them into harmony with the regulations for drugs.

- Eliminate the need for establishment license application for biologics.

- Eliminate the batch certification and monograph requirements for insulin and antibiotics.

- Streamline the approval processes for drug and biological manufacturing changes.

- Reduce the requirements for environmental assessment as part of a product application.

- Increase patient access to experimental drugs and medical devices.

- Accelerate review of important new medical products.

- Establish a database on clinical trials that will be accessible by patients.

INFORMATION ON OFF-LABEL USE AND ECONOMICS

The law abolishes the long-standing prohibition on dissemination by manufacturers of information about unapproved uses of drugs and medical devices. The act allows a firm to disseminate peer-reviewed journal articles about an off-label indication of its product, provided the company follows specific guidelines established by the FDA. Drug companies are also allowed to provide economic information about their products, under specific FDA guidelines.

PHARMACY COMPOUNDING

The act creates a special exemption to ensure continued availability of compounded drug products prepared by pharmacists to provide patients with individualized therapies not available commercially. The law, however, seeks to prevent manufacturing under the guise of compounding by establishing parameters within which the practice is appropriate and lawful.

RISK-BASED REGULATION OF MEDICAL DEVICES

FDAMA enhances the FDA's recent measures to focus its device review resources on those medical devices that present the greatest risks to patients. For example, the law:

- Exempts from premarket notification Class I devices that are not intended for a use that is of substantial importance in preventing impairment of human health, or that do not present a potential unreasonable risk of illness or injury.

- Directs the FDA to focus its post-market surveillance on higher-risk devices.

- Allows the agency to implement a reporting system that concentrates on a representative sample of user facilities (for example, hospitals and nursing homes) that experience deaths and serious illnesses or injuries linked with the use of medical devices.

- Expands an ongoing pilot program under which the FDA accredits outside "third party" experts to conduct the initial review of all Class I and low-to-intermediate-risk Class II devices.

- Specifies that an accredited person may not review devices that are permanently implantable, life-supporting, life-sustaining, or for which clinical data are required.

STANDARDS FOR MEDICAL PRODUCTS

Although FDAMA reduces or simplifies many regulatory obligations of manufacturers, it does not lower the standards by which medical products are introduced into the marketplace. FDAMA:

- Codifies the agency's current practice of allowing, in certain circumstances, one clinical investigation as the basis for approval of a new drug or biologic; however, it does preserve the presumption that, as a general rule, two adequate and well-controlled studies are needed to prove safety and effectiveness.

- Specifies that the FDA may keep out of the market medical devices whose manufacturing processes are so deficient that they could present a serious health hazard.

- Gives the agency authority to take appropriate action if the technology of a device suggests that it is likely to be used for a potentially harmful unlabeled use.

Before going on to more detailed consideration of how to create and implement product development planning, it is important to understand how healthcare products are regulated in the United States under the provisions of FDAMA, and what is required for these products to be legally sold.

Whether a product is classified as a drug, biologic, or medical device is not always intuitively obvious. In fact, some products now defined as medical devices were previously classified as drugs. Biologics are also legally defined either as drugs or devices and are therefore also subject to the provisions relating to drugs or devices.[7] Biologics also are common components of medical devices, especially in vitro diagnostic devices, and in the marketplace, there is generally no perceived distinction between drugs and therapeutic biologics such as vaccines or blood clotting factors.

Despite some significant overlap in the attributes of each product category, a different suborganization, or center, within the FDA has been charged with primary responsibility for regulating each category. However, even the FDA has had to cry "uncle" and admit that in a substantial number of cases, there is a need for review by more than one center, even though only one center would have primary regulatory jurisdiction.

DRUGS AND BIOLOGICS

FDA Consolidation of Drugs and Biologics

In the marketplace, a distinction between drugs and many biologics is typically not made, and figures related to use or sales of both are often lumped together in the category of pharmaceuticals. Likewise, in terms of product development, the principles and challenges encountered in the two areas are often fundamentally the same. But the FDA was resistant to act on the similarities, and until the implementation of FDAMA, the FDA regulated biologics in a different manner than drugs. Although the agency recognized the similarities between the definitions of drugs and of biologics, the FDA position was that there were important differences between the two that required different regulatory processes. According to the FDA, a drug is typically a chemical entity that can be well-characterized with respect to its physical attributes, including its structure, whereas a biologic is typically a complex mixture of components that cannot be separated and characterized.

Before the implementation of FDAMA, the perceived inability to fully characterize final biological products led the FDA to require that the regulation of biologics rely heavily on in-process testing and validation of production. Thus, a significant difference between FDA approval processes for new drugs and biologics existed. Marketing a new drug in the United States required *approval* of a new drug application (NDA) for the drug *product*. In comparison, marketing of a biologics product required separate processes to obtain: (1) a *license* for the *biologic product* through approval of a product license application (PLA); and (2) a *license* for the *manufacturing facility* for the biologic through approval of an establishment license application (ELA). As a result of government reinvention and modernization efforts to minimize the review and approval of new biologics, the separate ELA has now been eliminated, and the PLA has been replaced by a single biologics license application (BLA). This move reflects a harmonization of biologics regulation with that of the NDA process for drugs.

In 2003, the FDA completed a consolidation of certain biologic product reviews from CBER to CDER, with the objective of producing a more efficient, effective, and consistent review program for drugs and biologics. The product categories that had previously been regulated by CBER as biologics that have been transferred to CDER include:

- Monoclonal antibodies intended for therapeutic use

- Cytokines, growth factors, enzymes, immunomodulators, and thrombolytics intended for therapeutic use

- Proteins intended for therapeutic use that are extracted from animals or microorganisms, including recombinant versions of these products (except clotting factors)

- Other non-vaccine therapeutic immunotherapies

Regardless of which FDA center has review jurisdiction, the safety, purity, potency, and efficacy of drugs and biologics must be established to the satisfaction of the FDA before a product will be approved for marketing.

Drugs. The FDA regulates prescription and over-the-counter medicines for humans through its Center for Drug Evaluation and Research (CDER). The primary responsibility of CDER is to approve the marketing of drugs that are effective for their labeled indications, provide benefits that outweigh their risks, are of high quality, and have directions for use that are complete and honestly communicated. The regulatory authority for drugs is contained in the FD&C Act, which defines drugs principally as "articles intended for use in the diagnosis, cure, mitigation, treatment, or prevention of disease in man or other animals . . . intended to affect the structure or any function of the body of man. . . ." (see Figure 2.1).[8]

Before a new drug product under development can be tested on humans, an investigational new drug (IND) application must be filed. The minimum information included in an IND is shown in Figure 2.2. In reviewing an IND, the FDA is most concerned with determining that adequate data have been provided to establish that the new product is reasonably safe to use on human subjects in clinical trials, and that the proposed clinical trial will generate useful and acceptable data. If the IND is approved, the first step has been taken in allowing the as yet unapproved drug to be evaluated in clinical trials (that is, trials on humans) without breaking the law. Clinical trials are performed with the consent of participating hospitals and institutions, and, upon the conclusion of a successful clinical trial, a new drug application (NDA) is submitted to the FDA for review. If the NDA is approved, a drug may be legally marketed.

The term "drug" means:

(A) articles recognized in the official United States Pharmacopoeia, official Homeopathic Pharmacopoeia of the United States, or official National Formulary, or any supplement to any of them; and

(B) articles intended for use in the diagnosis, cure, mitigation, treatment, or prevention of disease in man or other animals; and

(C) articles (other than food) intended to affect the structure or any function of the body of man or other animals; and

(D) articles intended for use as a component of any articles specified in clause (A), (B), or (C).

Figure 2.1   Definition of a drug.
Source: Federal Food, Drug, and Cosmetic Act

- Information about the sponsor and the investigators
- The name of the drug, the mechanism of action, the marketing history, and a brief description of the clinical trial
- A summary of all safety and clinical data
- A plan for clinical investigation
- A description of the drug composition, the method of manufacture of the drug, and quality control measures used in production
- A description of pharmacology and toxicology studies and results upon which the sponsor has determined it is reasonably safe to conduct clinical trials
- A summary of other previous use of the drug in humans
- Additional information, such as dependence/abuse potential or radioactive drug information

Figure 2.2   Minimum information included in an IND.

The term "bological product" (biologic) means:

any virus, therapeutic serum, toxin, antitoxin, vaccine, blood, blood component or derivative, allergenic product, or analogous product, or arsphenamine or its derivatives (or any other trivalent organic arsenic compound), applicable to the prevention, treatment, or cure of diseases or injuries of man.

Figure 2.3   Definition of a biological product.
Source: Public Health Service Act

Biologics. Biologics are medical preparations made from living organisms and their products; the category includes vaccines, blood products, certain diagnostic products, and biotechnology-derived products. The FDA's Center for Biologics Evaluation and Research (CBER) is responsible for ensuring the safety, efficacy, potency, and purity of biological products used to treat, prevent, or cure diseases. The center regards its mission as protection and enhancement of the public health through regulation of biological and related products according to statutory authorities, which for biologics resides both in the Public Health Service (PHS) Act and the FD&C Act. The PHS Act defines a biologic (also known as a biological product) as "any virus, therapeutic serum, toxin, antitoxin, vaccine, blood, blood component or derivative, allergenic product, or analogous product . . . applicable to the prevention, treatment, or cure of diseases or injuries of man. . . ." (see Figure 2.3).[9] As described earlier, there have been numerous and profound changes in the regulation of biologics. CBER, for the time being, will concentrate its expertise and effort in the areas of vaccines, blood safety, gene therapy, and tissue transplantation. Product classes that remain at CBER are:

- Viral-vectored gene insertions
- Products composed of human or animal cells or from physical parts of those cells
- Allergen patch tests
- Allergenics
- Antitoxins, antivenoms, and venoms
- Biological in vitro diagnostics
- Vaccines

- Toxoids and toxins intended for immunization
- Blood, blood components, and related products

Some biologics under CBER jurisdiction are classified by legal definition as devices (for example, blood collection accessories, diagnostic products containing biologic components). Biologic devices are regulated by CBER according to the requirements for medical devices.

MEDICAL DEVICES

Responsibility for ensuring the safety and effectiveness of medical devices and radiation-emitting products falls to the Center for Devices and Radiological Health (CDRH) of the FDA. There are thousands of types of medical devices, from heart pacemakers to wheelchairs, from in vitro diagnostics to the software that controls automated devices. Ultrasound and X-ray machines, surgical lasers, and video display terminals used with medical equipment are examples of radiation-emitting medical devices.

Even though all of these medical devices fall under the jurisdiction of CDRH, the vagaries of FDA guidelines and regulations can make dealing with this category of healthcare products a nightmare. A bit of history might help explain some of the confusion and complexity.

Although the Act of 1938 gave the FDA the authority to regulate medical devices in order to assure their safety, the FDA found itself in a position, familiar to everyone in middle management, of having a great deal of responsibility but insufficient authority to meet the demands of the responsibility. A medical device, defined by the legislation as "any instrument, apparatus, or contrivance, including any of its components or parts, intended for use in the diagnosis, cure, treatment, or prevention of disease in man or other animals," could be marketed virtually at whim, whether or not it worked or was safe to use. If a device was determined to be in violation of the Act—if it was considered adulterated or included any filthy, putrid, or decomposed substance, or if it was prepared, packed, or held under unsanitary conditions—the FDA could seize the product. It could also request an injunction against its production, distribution, or use, and could even recommend criminal prosecution of the manufacturer or other responsible parties. What the FDA could not do, however, was require any kind of testing or approval of medical devices *before* they were marketed. Yet a 1962 amendment to the Act *did* expand testing requirements for new drugs and gave the FDA the authority to require premarket approval for drugs.

As years went by and technological advances took medical devices into the realm of highly sophisticated, often invasive products that could have life-or-death impact on the health and safety of a patient, it became clear that the FDA didn't have the teeth it needed to accomplish its mission. Problems with some of these critical devices were recognized as having led to numerous patient injuries, and some of the injuries led to deaths.

In 1970, a government panel (chaired by then Assistant Secretary of the Department of Health, Education, and Welfare Theodore Cooper), was given the responsibility of reviewing the regulation of medical devices. The Cooper committee findings indicated that 10,000 injuries related to medical devices had occurred over a 10-year period, and that 751 of the injuries resulted in death. Specific examples disclosed by the Cooper committee included during that 10-year period were:

- 300 injuries and 512 deaths attributed to heart valves

- 186 injuries and 89 deaths attributed to pacemakers

- 8000 injuries and 10 deaths attributed to intrauterine devices[10]

Confronted with these dual issues of safety and efficacy, the courts ruled that certain medical devices were, in fact, drugs and could therefore be regulated as such. In other words, the FDA could require testing and approval of these critical devices-turned-drugs before they were marketed.

In 1976, the Medical Device Amendments to the Act was signed into law, providing the FDA with authority to regulate devices during most phases of their development, testing, production, distribution, and use. The Safe Medical Devices Act (SMDA) of 1990 increased the authority of the FDA with regard to medical devices and added such things as design validation, recall authority, tracking requirements, and civil penalties to the laundry list over which the FDA has power.

As shown in Figure 2.4, a medical device is now, and until further notice, defined as "an instrument, apparatus, implement, machine, contrivance, implant, in vitro reagent, or other similar or related article, including any component, part, or accessory . . , which is intended for use in the diagnosis . . , cure, mitigation, treatment, or prevention of disease . . , and which does not achieve its primary intended purposes through chemical action within or on the body . . , and which is not dependent upon being metabolized for the achievement of any of its primary intended purposes."[11]

The final portion of the definition is what delineates the distinction between devices and drugs. In reality though, it is not always easy to determine whether or not a chemical action takes place that influences the action of a medical device, or whether metabolic products of absorbable devices contribute to efficacy. Furthermore, there is a distinct incentive for device manufacturers not to look for the answer, since any finding that the efficacy of a device is based on physiology or biochemistry could lead

The term "device" means:

an instrument, apparatus, implement, machine, contrivance, implant, in vitro reagent, or other similar or related article, including any component, part, or accessory, which is

(A) recognized in the official National Formulary, or the United States Pharmacopoeia, or any supplement to them,

(B) intended for use in the diagnosis of disease or other conditions, or in the cure, mitigation, treatment, or prevention of disease, in man or other animals, or

(C) intended to affect the structure or any function of the body of man or other animals, and which does not achieve its primary intended purposes through chemical action within or on the body of man or other animals and which is not dependent upon being metabolized for the achievement of its primary intended purposes.

Figure 2.4 Definition of medical device.
Source: Federal Food, Drug, and Cosmetic Act

to reclassification of the device as a drug or biologic. And that is something device manufacturers do not want.

More than 1700 major types of medical devices are regulated by CDRH. Many of these devices may be marketed in the United States without FDA review. The FDA grants some medical devices clearance to be commercially distributed or marketed through a process known as *premarket notification* [510(k)]. Other devices must be taken through a more stringent process known as *premarket approval* (PMA). If clinical testing of a new device is required, an investigational device exemption (IDE), which is analogous to an IND, must generally be filed with the FDA. Like an IND, an approved IDE provides a manufacturer the opportunity to legally establish the safety and effectiveness in humans of a new product, which has not yet been approved or cleared for marketing, through clinical studies on human subjects. The type of information included in an IDE is given in Figure 2.5. The similarities between an IND and an IDE are readily apparent.

As one might expect, regulating the large and diverse group of products known as *medical devices* is difficult. Accordingly, the review and clearance or approval processes for medical devices range from complicated to baffling.

Data on recent submissions and approval or clearance activities of CDER, CBER, and CDRH are summarized in Tables 2.2, 2.3, and 2.4.

- Information about the sponsor
- A complete report of prior investigations of the device, including clinical, animal, and laboratory testing; a bibliography of all publications; and a summary of all unpublished information
- An investigational plan
- A description of methods, facilities, and controls used for the manufacture and (if appropriate) installation of the device
- Information about investigators and institutions where investigations will be conducted
- Any other relevant information requested by the FDA

Figure 2.5 Minimum information included in an IDE.

Table 2.2 Major drug review activity.

Type of Submission	Number of Submissions Received		
	CY 2000	CY 2001	CY 2002
Original NDAs received	115	99	109
NDAs approved	98	66	78
Original INDs received	1815	1872	2374

Source: U.S. Department of Health and Human Services, Public Health Service, Food and Drug Administration, Center for Drug Evaluation and Research, *CDER Report to the Nation 2002*

Table 2.3 Major biologics review activities.

Submission	FY 2000	FY2001	FY 2002
Product applications received	84	18	18
Product applications approved	56	24	23
INDs/IDEs* received	674	611	528

*IDEs for biological devices
Source: CBER Annual Report FY 2002

Specific examples of new drugs, biologics, and medical devices that have recently received approval or clearance for marketing are given in Tables 2.5, 2.6, and 2.7.

Table 2.4 Major medical device submissions received by CDRH.

Type of Submission	Number of Submissions Received		
	FY 2000	FY 2001	FY 2002
Original PMAs	67	71	48
PMA supplements	546	641	644
510(k)s	4202	4248	4230
Original IDEs	311	284	312

Source: U.S. Department of Health and Human Services, Public Health Service, Food and Drug Administration, Center for Devices and Radiological Health, *Office of Device Evaluations Annual Report Fiscal Year 2002* (2002)

Table 2.5 Recent new molecular entities approved by CDER.*

Generic Name	Trade Name	Applicant
Enfuvirtide	Fuzeon	Roche
Pegvisomant	Somavert	Pharmacia and Upjohn
Aprepitant	Emend	Merck
Gemifloxacin Mesylate	Factive	LG Life
Gefitinib	Iressa	AstraZeneca
Bortezomib	Velcade	Millennium Pharms
Ibandronate Sodium	Boniva	Roche
Alfuzosin Hydrochloride	Uroxatral	Sanofi-Synthelabo
Atazanavir Sulfate	Reyataz	Bristol Myers Squibb
Sodium Oxybate	Xyrem	Orphan Medical
Tegaserod Maleate	Zelnorm	Novartis
Oxaliplatin	Eloxatin	Sanofi
Adefovir Dipivoxil	Hepsera	Gilead
Eplerenone	Inspra	GD Searle
Ezetimibe	Zetia	MSP Singapore
Aripiprazole	Abilify	Otsuka
Nitazoxanide	Alinia	Romark
Atomoxetine Hydrochloride	Strattera	Lilly
Icodextrin	Extraneal	Baxter Healthcare
Eletriptan Hydrobromide	Relpax	Pfizer

* New molecular entities (NMEs), also known as new chemical entities (NCEs), are new drugs that contain an active substance that has never before been approved for marketing in any form in the United States.

Source: CDER

Table 2.6 Some recent BLA approvals.

Trade Name/ Proper Name	Indication for Use	Manufacturer/ License No.
Amevive Alefacept	Treatment of adult patients with moderate to severe chronic plaque psoriasis who are candidates for systemic therapy or phototherapy	Biogen, Inc.
Source Plasma	For further manufacturing	International BioResources, LLC
Crosseal Fibrin Sealant (Human)	Adjunct to hemostasis in patients undergoing liver surgery, when control of bleeding by conventional surgical techniques is ineffective or impractical	OMRIX Biopharmaceuticals, Ltd.
ORTHO Antibody to HBsAG ELISA Test System 3 Antibody to Hepatitis B Surface Antigen (Mouse Monoclonal) Enzyme-Linked Immunosorbent Assay (ELISA)	Detection of hepatitis B surface antigen in human serum or plasma as a screening test and an aid in the diagnosis of potential hepatitis B infection	Ortho-Clinical Diagnostics, Inc.
Fabrazyme Agalsidase beta	For use in patients with Fabry disease to reduce globotriaosylceramide (GL-3) deposition in capillary endothelium of the kidney and certain other cell types	Genzyme Corp.
FluMist Influenza Virus Vaccine, Live, Intranasal	For active immunization for the prevention of disease caused by influenza A and B viruses in healthy children and adolescents, 5–17 years of age, and healthy adults, 18–49 years of age	MedImmune Vaccines, Inc.
Xolair Omalizumab	For adults and adolescents (12 years of age and above) with moderate to severe persistent asthma who have a positive skin test or *in vitro* reactivity to a perennial aeroallergen and whose symptoms are inadequately controlled with inhaled corticosteroids	Genentech, Inc.

continued

continued

Trade Name/ Proper Name	Indication for Use	Manufacturer/ License No.
Bexxar Tositumomab and Iodine I-131 Tositumomab	Treatment of patients with CD20 positive, follicular, non-Hodgkin's lymphoma, with and without transformation, whose disease is refractory to Rituximab and has relapsed following chemotherapy	Corixa Corp.
Zemaira Alpha-1-Proteinase Inhibitor (Human)	Chronic augmentation and maintenance therapy in individuals with alpha1-proteinase inhibitor deficiency and evidence of emphysema	Aventis Behring LLC
Advate Antihemophilic Factor (Recombinant), Plasma/Albumin Free Method (rAHF-PFM)	Indicated in hemophilia A (classical hemophilia) for the prevention and control of bleeding episodes. Antihemophilic Factor (Recombinant), Plasma/ Albumin Free Method is also indicated in the perioperative management of patients with hemophilia A.	Baxter Healthcare Corp.

Source: CBER

THE NEW FDA

In addition to the previously described changes resulting from the implementation of FDAMA, the FDA has taken on a new look in a variety of areas. The years 2002 and 2003 alone marked significant developments.

New Leadership

A new commissioner, Dr. Mark McClellan, was appointed to head the FDA following a two-year period in which the position had been vacant, and a new director stepped into place at CBER.

Office of Combination Products

The FDA established an Office of Combination Products (OCP) to streamline the regulatory pathway for complex drug-device, drug-biologic, and

Table 2.7 Recent device actions.

(a) Examples of 2003 Device PMA Original Approvals

Device Trade Name	Manufacturer	Device Description/ Indications
FX miniRAIL RX Percutaneous Transluminal Coronary Angioplasty (PTCA) Catheter	X Technologies, Inc.	For balloon dilatation of the stenotic portion of a coronary artery, including in-stent restenosis, for the purpose of improving myocardial perfusion
ThinPrep Imaging System	Cytyc Corporation	Device for assisting in primary cervical cancer screening of ThinPrep Pap Test slides
Cypher Drug-Eluting Stent	Cordis Corporation	Drug-eluting coronary stent to reduce rate of reblockage following angioplasty
Bayer Versant HCV RNA 3.0 Assay	Bayer Diagnostics	Signal amplification nucleic acid probe assay for the quantitation of human hepatitis C viral RNA (HCV RNA) in the serum or plasma of HCV-infected individuals using the Bayer System 340 bDNA Analyzer.
FemCap Barrier Contraceptive	FemCap, Inc.	Indicated for use by women of childbearing age who desire to prevent or postpone pregnancy

(b) Examples of 2003 substantially equivalent device 510(k) decisions

Device	Manufacturer
West Nile Virus IgM Capture ELISA	PanBio Limited
Mid Stream Pregnancy Test	Advanced Diagnostics, Inc.
MIIG II Bone Graft Substitute	Wright Medical Technology, Inc.
XYLOS XCELL Antimicrobial Dressing	Xylos Corporation
CPT 12/14 Hip Prostheses	Zimmer, Inc.

Source: CDRH

device-biologic combination products (see Figure 2.6). As medical product technologies became more sophisticated, the FDA faced a major and confounding issue in establishing which review center—CDER, CBER, or CDRH—had jurisdiction for the regulation of such products, and there were more than a few intercenter turf battles. The new office has responsibility for the complete regulatory cycle of combination products, including jurisdiction decisions. OCP will assign a combination product to an FDA center for primary jurisdiction; oversee the timeliness and coordination of

As defined in 21 CFR§ 3.2(e), the term combination product includes:

(1) A product comprised of two or more regulated components, i.e., drug/device, biologic/device, drug/biologic, or drug/device/biologic, that are physically, chemically, or otherwise combined or mixed and produced as a single entity;

(2) Two or more separate products packaged together in a single package or as a unit and comprised of drug and device products, device and biological products, or biological and drug products;

(3) A drug, device, or biological product packaged separately that according to its investigational plan or proposed labeling is intended for use only with an approved individually specified drug, device, or biological product where both are required to achieve the intended use, indication, or effect and where upon approval of the proposed product the labeling of the approved product would need to be changed, e.g., to reflect a change in intended use, dosage form, strength, route of administration, or significant change in dose; or

(4) Any investigational drug, device, or biological product packaged separately that according to its proposed labeling is for use only with another individually specified investigational drug, device, or biological product where both are required to achieve the intended use, indication, or effect.

Figure 2.6   Definition of a combination product.
Source: CDRH, Office of Combination Products

reviews involving more than one center; resolve disputes regarding review issues; and review and modify, revise, or even eliminate agreements, guidance documents, or practices, as the office deems appropriate for a specific combination product. Examples of combination products include:

- Drug-eluting cardiovascular stents
- Lumber-tapered fusion devices with genetically engineered human protein
- Dental prophylaxis pastes with drug components
- Human dermal collagen implants for aesthetic use

MDUFMA

The Medical Device User Fee and Modernization Act of 2002 (MDUFMA) amends the FD&C Act to grant CDRH new responsibilities and resources, including collection of user fees for premarket review of medical devices. These fees are analogous to the PDUFA fees discussed earlier.

Increased Surveillance of Medical Devices

The FDA announced that it will require manufacturers of certain critical medical devices to conduct post-market surveillance on those products. The devices are those for which failure would reasonably be expected to cause severe adverse consequences. This surveillance will provide a way for the FDA (and manufacturers) to identify problems that were not identified during the course of product development.

Approval of Some Products Based on Animal Data

The FDA has amended drug and biologics regulations to allow approval of certain drugs and biologics, specifically some products intended to reduce or prevent serious or life-threatening conditions, without requiring human clinical trials for efficacy. If studies on humans are not ethical or feasible, the agency may accept animal efficacy data in lieu of human clinical trials data. The new rule reflects the unfortunate state of the human condition, in that FDA regards it as especially applicable to therapies used to reduce or prevent the toxicity of chemical, biological, radiological, or nuclear weapons agents.

Electronic Submissions

A proposal was issued by FDA for the first agency regulation to require submission of information by electronic means. This first step would apply to submission of certain labeling for certain drugs and biologics applications.

Risk-Based Approach to Pharmaceuticals Manufacturing

The FDA announced that it is undertaking an initiative called "Pharmaceutical cGMPs for the 21st Century: A Risk-Based Approach" to integrate science-based risk management with integrated quality control systems. The purpose of the endeavor is to direct resources to ensure that drug and biologics manufacturing will better serve the cause of patient safety. The agency will match its level of effort against the magnitude of possible risk associated with a product and its manufacturing. This will increase the level of responsibility for manufacturers of high-risk products, while alleviating some burden for manufacturers of low-risk products.

Withdrawal of Outdated Draft Proposals

The FDA announced plans to withdraw 84 old proposed actions and rules that were never finalized and that are no longer regarded as agency priorities. There were so many proposed rules and other actions that had never been finalized or had never been implemented, that the administrative requirements and review backlog became unmanageable by the FDA. The move is expected to clarify the status of old projects, simplify and streamline FDA's rulemaking process, and focus agency resources on more relevant proposals. Withdrawing a proposal doesn't preclude the FDA from reissuing the same, or similar proposal in the future. Some of the documents related to drugs, biologics, and medical devices are shown in Table 2.8.

One important point for those unaccustomed to or uninitiated in regulatory matters is that despite FDA efforts to streamline regulatory processes, a company does not obtain FDA clearance or approval to market a new healthcare product by simply filling out an application form. Submitting the documentation for a 510(k), PMA, NDA, or BLA is not like applying for a loan or a driver's license. Depending upon the product, these submissions may range in length from less than 100 pages (for example, for some medical devices) to hundreds of thousands of pages (for example, for some drugs with extensive clinical data).

While there is not a straightforward application form specifically appropriate for each general class of products (devices or drugs or biologics), there is a general format concerning the minimum information and data that the FDA expects to see in each type of submission for approval or clearance. The FDA has generated voluminous quantities of guidance and regulations publications pertaining to specific categories of regulated healthcare products. Regulations applicable to drugs, biologics, and medical devices will continue to change and evolve in response to technical developments, market urgency, and political pressures. Direct consultation with the FDA, attention to the guidance documents, and strict adherence to issued regulations will contribute to the definition of the structure and substance of a particular submission.

Table 2.8 Some outdated proposals and other actions that FDA plans to withdraw.

Title	Publication Date
Radioactive Drugs, Including Biological Products	July 25, 1975
Medical Devices; Sponges for Internal Use	November 28, 1976
Medical Devices; Classification of Powered Myoelectric Biofeedback Equipment	August 28, 1979
New Drug and Antibiotic Application Review; Proposed User Charge	August 6, 1985
Hematology and Pathology Devices; Premarket Approval of the Automated Blood Cell Separator Intended for Routine Collection of Blood and Blood Components	February 19, 1988
Current Good Manufacturing Practices for Blood and Blood Components; Proficiency Testing Requirements	June 6, 1989
Reclassification of Electroconvulsive Therapy	September 15, 1990
Use of Aseptic Processing and Terminal Sterilization in the Preparation of Sterile Pharmaceuticals for Human and Veterinary Use	October 11, 1991
Cardiovascular Devices; Effective Date of Requirement for PMA of Nonroller-Type Cardiopulmonary Bypass Blood Pump	July 6, 1993
Dental Devices; Effective Date of Requirement for Premarket Approval of Partially Fabricated Denture Kits	November 29, 1995

Source: Food and Drug Administration, 21 CFR Chapter 1, Docket no. 02N-0434 (10 April 2003)

3

Product Liability and Product Development

The operation was a success, but the patient died.

—Unknown

In law nothing is certain but expense.

—Samuel Butler

Pharmaceutical and medical device industries are major targets of product liability litigation. The very nature of these products makes them vulnerable to litigation, in no small part because:

- Many devices and drugs are used in the treatment of patients who are already ill or injured.

- These products may be used in procedures that are invasive or otherwise inherently risky.

- Drugs and devices are often used in life-or-death situations, in which a product-related risk is recognized but deemed by medical professionals to be outweighed by benefit.

- By their very definition, drugs and medical devices are intended to affect the structure or function of the body.

Unintended and/or unexpected consequences of the use, overuse, or misuse of drugs and medical devices include other illness, injury, abnormal behavior, brain damage, and death. Sometimes an adverse event occurs often enough and is consistent enough to be clearly associated with a product; frequently, there appears to be a correlation, but compelling evidence that the product caused harm is lacking. In either case, a patient is harmed, and by coincidence or not, the product was used on the patient prior to the occurrence of the harm.

The penalties associated with product liability findings are a nightmare for medical products manufacturers. Manufacturers and sellers have been required to pay staggering amounts of money to patients for damages or injuries suffered because of product defects. A few examples of some recent headline-grabbers are shown in Table 3.1. Product liability lawsuits can also have a significant negative effect on the resources, reputation, and value of a company.

There is a conceit within some organizations that FDA clearance or approval of a product for marketing confers immunity to product liability. Wrong. In fact, while product liability actions sometimes arise during pre-approval clinical trials for a product, most product liability exposure occurs after the product is on the market—which means *after* regulatory requirements have been met. It is important to recognize that FDA regulation is intended to be separate from the civil liability process.

For many years, though, medical device manufacturers were essentially protected from liability for devices that had received marketing clearance or approval from the FDA because of an interpretation of certain provisions of the Medical Device Amendments of 1976. The free ride ended with a watershed decision by the U.S. Supreme Court in 1996, which established that consumers injured by certain faulty medical devices can seek damages against the manufacturer under state law, even if the devices comply with FDA regulations.[12] In other words, the federal law does not preempt state law with regard to certain medical device product liability.

Table 3.1   Examples of recent U.S. national class action product liability settlements.

Product	Purpose	Settlement (Approximate)
Redux, Pondimin (Fen-Phen)	Weight control	$ 3.75 billion
Inter-OP, Natural Knee	Hip replacement Knee replacement	$ 1 billion
Baycol	Cholesterol reduction	Possibly > $2 billion*

* As of May 2003, company had settled 740 suits for $219 million, and had approximately 8600 additional personal injury suits pending in the United States.

While the Supreme Court ruling on the case at point applies to devices cleared for marketing under the provisions of 510(k) Premarket Notification, the principles have since been successfully applied to devices approved by the FDA through the PMA process.[13]

There is no explicit federal preemption provision for pharmaceutical products, which seriously weakens any hope for protection of therapeutic products from civil suits. Consequently, drug and biologics manufacturers can be easy targets for state tort liability.

BASIS OF PRODUCT LIABILITY

Product liability may be established by evidence that the product causing the harm was not reasonably fit, suitable, or safe for its intended purpose because of design defects, warning defects, or manufacturing defects (see Figure 3.1).[14]

A product:

(a) contains a *manufacturing defect* when the product departs from its intended design even though all possible care was exercised in the preparation and marketing of the product;

(b) is *defective in design* when the foreseeable risks of harm posed by the product could have been reduced or avoided by the adoption of a reasonable alternative design by the seller or other distributor, or a predecessor in the commercial chain of distribution, and the omission of the alternative design renders the product not reasonably safe;

(c) is defective because of *inadequate instructions or warnings* when the foreseeable risks of harm posed by the product could have been reduced or avoided by the provision of reasonable instructions or warnings by the seller or other distributor, or a predecessor in the commercial chain of distribution, and the omission of the instructions or warnings renders the product not reasonably safe.

Figure 3.1   Establishing product defects for product liability.
Source: Restatement (Third) of Torts: Prod. Liab. §2 (1998)

Design Defects

A product design may be inherently dangerous or may be designed in a manner that is prone to failure in a way that can cause harm. Some products may exacerbate preexisting injuries or illnesses of patients. Properly executed product development activities, such as application of design controls and attention to human factors, are crucial in minimizing the occurrence of design defects.

Warning Defects

Any known or reasonably anticipated hazard associated with the use of a medical product should be made clear and obvious in the labeling and in instructions for use. Although many medical professionals and/or patients make no attempt to read package inserts and other labeling, a manufacturer has a duty to minimize known or foreseeable risks through effective warnings that clearly convey:

- The nature of the hazard
- The level of the hazard
- Consequences of the hazard
- The means to avoid the hazard

Product development teams must be able to accurately and effectively communicate the required information to those within their company who are responsible for labeling development.

Manufacturing Defects

Even the most well-designed, well-labeled product is a lawsuit incubator if it has not been manufactured according to the manufacturer's specifications. This includes design specifications and manufacturing process specifications. Deviation from specifications during manufacturing may produce a product that may malfunction or otherwise be dangerous. Those involved in product development typically have limited influence on post-launch manufacturing of a marketed product.

THE ROLE OF PRODUCT DEVELOPMENT

With the likely exception of manufacturing defects, product development has a central obligation in the prevention of product liability. To avoid product

Design for foreseeable risks. Gain adequate familiarity with the environment in which the product is intended to be used, and have the imagination to anticipate when, where, how, why, and by whom the products are reasonably likely to be misused.

Test the product. Sufficient early prototype or product testing can reveal defects and deficiencies.

Assess the risk of injury. Conduct risk analysis with a multifunctional team to cover as many aspects of product use and foreseeable misuse as possible.

Communicate findings. Clearly inform decision makers about risks and means to avoid or minimize the risks.

Figure 3.2 Responsibilities of product development planning in minimizing future product liability problems.

liability, the risk of a product causing harm must be minimized. To this end, as shown in Figure 3.2, responsibilities and goals for product development teams include the following:

1. *Design for foreseeable risks.* This means having adequate familiarity with the environment in which the product is intended to be used, and having the imagination to anticipate when, where, how, why, and by whom the products are reasonably likely to be misused.

2. *Test the product.* Sufficient early prototype or product testing can reveal defects and deficiencies.

3. *Assess the risk of injury.* Conduct risk analysis with a multifunctional team to cover as many aspects of product use and foreseeable misuse as possible.

Processes for achieving these objectives are discussed throughout this book.

If these steps result in the identification of safety risks that may be associated with the normal use of the product or with foreseeable misuse of the product, important decisions will fall on the shoulders of the product development team. Questions that will need to be addressed and resolved are:

1. Have all of the safety risks been identified for normal use of the product?

2. Have all of the safety risks been identified for foreseeable misuse of the product?

3. To what extent are the identified risks minimized through routine design development procedures, product testing, and application of industry standards?

4. To what extent will warnings and anticipated adherence to those warnings minimize the hazard?

5. Is an alternative, lower-risk design an alternative?

6. Given the identified risks of the product, do you, the manufacturer, consider the product to be reasonably safe?

Many products can be made safer through extensive design changes, but no product can be made foolproof and guaranteed as safe. The finesse is in determining whether the new product in question is safe enough to take to market, based on the multifunctional analysis of risk. This, in turn, creates a risky situation for the product development team, so any decision should be reviewed and authorized by a level of management higher than the highest ranking team member. (Risk analysis is discussed in chapter 6.)

Product development is not just about the FDA and sales revenues. It is first and foremost about the well-being of patients. Any medical product being developed must, of course, comply with applicable industry standards and regulatory requirements, and must not be demonstrably less safe than comparable competitive products (Figure 3.3).

FDA approval of a product means the FDA believes that it is reasonably safe and effective for its labeled indications under its labeled conditions of use, but does not suggest an absence of risk. Rather, for purposes of marketing approval, the FDA considers a product to be reasonably safe

---

1. The well-being of patients

2. Compliance with regulatory requirements

3. Compliance with applicable industry standards

4. Providing safety and efficacy not less than competitive products

5. Creating value for the company

Figure 3.3 Primary considerations for product development planning.

if the clinical significance and probability of beneficial effects outweigh the likelihood and medical importance of its harmful or undesirable effects. In other words, a product is considered safe if it has a positive benefit/risk balance on a population and individual patient level.

The fact that compliance with government and industry regulations standards or practice does not automatically result in a design being reasonably safe is never an excuse for lack of compliance. The failure of a medical products manufacturer to comply with FDA regulations is neither permissible, nor ethical, nor good business. So don't skimp on product testing or on risk analysis exercises, which are discussed elsewhere in this book. Both can reveal nonobvious product defects. Diligence in those processes can help to keep your company out of court.

Part II

Bringing a New
Medical Product
to Market

4

Overview of the Approval Processes for Drugs, Biologics, and Medical Devices

We are all pilgrims on the same journey—but some pilgrims have better road maps.

—Nelson DeMille

In high art and in pure science detail is everything.

—Vladimir Nabokov

Now that the basics applicable to medical products and their regulation have been covered, it is time for a more detailed description of the actual process of product approval.

Product development planning encompasses the evaluation of product opportunities at all stages of development, from both internal and external origin. Too frequently, those who are responsible for regulatory and clinical activities for medical product manufacturers are excluded (willingly, unwillingly, or indifferently) from other areas of product development operations until someone determines that a new product is ready to be presented to the FDA. This is unfortunate, since even the most clever and productive scientists, the most clever and productive marketing managers, and the most clever and productive production managers will be thwarted if they don't have a fundamental concept of what is required for eventual approval or clearance for marketing. Without early regulatory and clinical involvement during product development planning, progress on developing a potentially valuable new product can come to a dead halt.

Significant consideration must be given to all regulatory and clinical pathways that remain before a product can be legally marketed, and if these requirements have been completed, to the strength and reliability of the information that has been generated. An intelligent assessment of time to market, cost to develop, and product use–associated risk requires an understanding of the regulatory road ahead. This chapter is especially targeted to those involved in product development who are not clinical or regulatory specialists.

DRUGS

Before a new drug can be marketed in the United States, it must receive approval from the FDA CDER, based on data demonstrating that the drug is safe and effective for its intended use. For a new drug—especially for a new chemical entity (NCE), which is an active drug substance that has never been previously approved by the FDA—the journey from a gleam in a scientist's eye to FDA approval is arduous, long, costly, and complicated. There are a number of ways in which the approval of some products can be hastened. In addition to understanding the categorization of potential new products, those involved in product development planning should not overlook any possibility that a product is eligible for a more rapid review process. Conversely, care must be taken not to mistakenly assume that a product is eligible or to misunderstand just what is implied in pursuing one of the available options. These are options and are not mandatory even if a product qualifies. The processes for fast-track designation, accelerated development, and priority review apply to products that would be a significant improvement in the treatment, diagnosis, or prevention of a serious or life-threatening disease. Each program carries its own risk, and manufacturers of this type of product need to examine all potential regulatory and clinical pathways.

Screening

The journey begins with laboratory investigations to identify possible candidate substances. Expert scientific and medical researchers try to conceptualize a target of action that might be effective in preventing, curing, or treating a disease. Thousands of compounds that have the potential of interacting with that biological target are screened in laboratory tests before a promising candidate substance is found. The candidates are extensively tested in preliminary laboratory studies to evaluate toxicity and pharmacologic effects. Most of the promising candidate drugs fall by the wayside because of obstacles encountered in these early steps.[15]

Preclinical Testing

With few exceptions, new drugs must be shown to be safe and effective in human subjects before FDA approval can be considered (the FDA can make exceptions to the clinical trial requirement for lifesaving drugs if testing in humans is unfeasible or unethical). The drug company must first convince the FDA that the drug is reasonably safe to use in humans to evaluate safety and efficacy in clinical trials. This is established through preclinical (that is, nonhuman) laboratory testing, including testing in animals. The FDA has guidelines and some regulations regarding the type of data and results it expects to see for a new drug before considering testing on humans, but the agency generally does not tell the drug company outright what specific laboratory evaluations or animal tests to run. As a result, the drug company often spends substantial time writing proposals and having discussions and meetings with the FDA to identify a mutually acceptable preclinical program.

Preclinical testing can be very expensive. A study program can range from hundreds of thousands of dollars to tens of millions of dollars, depending on the nature of the drug and on the availability of earlier safety and efficacy information.

Investigational New Drug Application

When preclinical testing satisfies the sponsor that the product is reasonably safe to move on to human trials, the company provides the data, along with manufacturing information and the proposed clinical protocol, and files an IND with the FDA. The IND is essentially a request for permission to ship the new and as yet unapproved drug to the test sites and to evaluate it in humans. If the FDA allows the IND, the company can proceed with clinical trials in humans. It is estimated that only five in 5000 drugs that enter preclinical testing advance to human trials.[16]

Clinical Trials

The purpose of all of the investigations, studies, and FDA filings described previously is to provide the foundation to justify that it is reasonably safe to test the new drug in humans in clinical trials designed to show the safety and effectiveness of the drug in the prevention, treatment, or cure of a disease. The results of the clinical trials are the most important factor in the ultimate approval or disapproval of a new drug. Clinical trials are discussed in chapter 9.

New Drug Application

If the drug company determines that the data from the clinical trials successfully demonstrate the safety and effectiveness of the new drug, an NDA is submitted to the FDA. An NDA, which commonly will be 100,000 pages or more, contains all of the scientific information that the company has gathered on the drug; statistical analyses of safety and efficacy data; detailed manufacturing information; information on packaging, stability, labeling; patent information; and more. The FDA reviews the NDA and ultimately makes a decision on whether the drug is approvable. Before making the decision, the agency will call on an advisory committee of outside experts to seek a committee opinion on the approvability of the drug. The recommendations of an advisory committee are not binding, but the agency considers them very carefully when making approval decisions. Figure 4.1 shows the mean approval time (the time from first NDA submission to NDA approval) for drugs.

Drug manufacturers must pay a fee to the FDA for review of NDA submissions, as stipulated by PDUFA.[17]

Inspections

If all previous steps have been found acceptable, the FDA inspects the manufacturing plant to ensure that the company is manufacturing the drug in compliance with FDA current good manufacturing practices (cGMP) regulations. Assuming satisfactory results, the FDA approves the drug for marketing in the United States.

As mentioned earlier, only five in 5000 compounds that enter preclinical testing are advanced to human testing in clinical trials. Of those entering clinical trials, only one in five receive FDA approval for marketing. The total cost incurred by an innovator/pioneer drug company for discovering and developing a new drug is estimated to be more than $800 million, taking into account both out-of-pocket costs, investment income foregone as a result of research and development expenditures before any returns are realized, and costs of failed projects. The total time required for discovery and development of a new drug by an innovator/pioneer drug company has been estimated to be 10 to 15 years.[18]

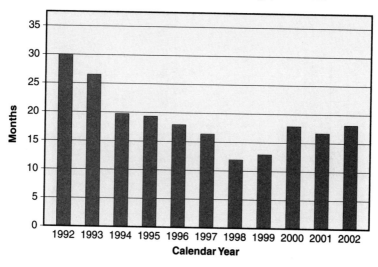

Mean Approval Times for New Drugs, 1992–2002

Figure 4.1 Drug approval time.*

* Approval time is the time from first NDA submission to NDA approval. It includes the sum of: FDA review time for the first submission of an NDA to the agency, plus any subsequent time during which a pharmaceutical sponsor addresses deficiencies in the NDA and resubmits the application, plus subsequent FDA review time.

Source: FDA, New Drug Approvals in 2002, PhRMA

BIOLOGICS

The clinical development and approval process for therapeutic biologics follows the same general pathway as for drugs. A sponsor who wishes to begin clinical trials on a biological product must submit an IND to FDA. Because biologics are derived from living organisms, and therefore are particularly at risk for immunogenicity, the IND will include information about the product's ability to elicit a protective immune response in animal testing. There also may be issues related to exclusion, destruction, or inactivation of pathogens that have the potential of being present in the source organism, organ, tissue, and so on. Rather than submitting an NDA, a biologics manufacturer files a *biologics license application* (BLA) for review, and with luck, for approval to market the new biologic. The mean approval time for biologics is shown in Figure 4.2. Biologics manufacturers also must pay PDUFA fees to the FDA for review of a BLA.

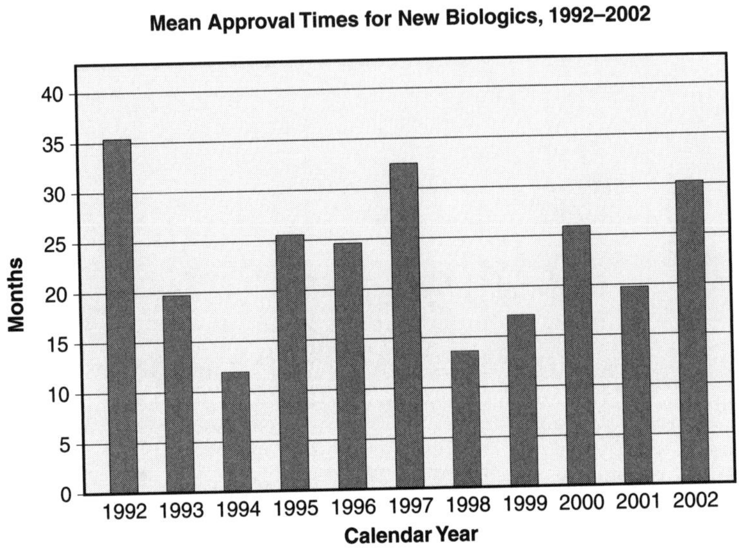

Mean Approval Times for New Biologics, 1992–2002

Figure 4.2 Mean approval times for new biologics.*

* Approval time is the time from the first application submission to approval. It includes the sum of: FDA review time for the first submission to the agency, plus any subsequent time during which a sponsor addresses deficiencies and resubmits the application, plus subsequent FDA review time.

Source: New Drug Approvals in 2002, PhRMA

GENERIC DRUGS AND ABBREVIATED NEW DRUG APPLICATIONS

The first version of a drug product that is approved by the FDA is known as an innovator or pioneer drug. A generic drug is comparable to an innovator drug in dosage form, strength, route of administration, quality, performance characteristics, and intended use. There are specific patent-related issues that apply to the approval and marketing of generic drugs.

Generic drug manufacturers submit an *abbreviated new drug application* (ANDA) to the Office of Generic Drugs at CDER. These applications are called "abbreviated" because the generic drug manufacturers are not required to include preclinical or clinical data to establish safety and effectiveness, since those attributes were already established by the manufacturer of the innovator drug through the NDA process. Rather, an ANDA must provide information and data demonstrating that the drug product is bioequivalent to the innovator drug and that the proposed use and labeling is identical to that of the reference innovator drug except for differences based on such things as manufacturer identity, tablet size or shape, distributor, and so on. Generic drug manufacturing plants are subject to the same inspection requirements that apply to manufacturers of new innovator drugs. Generic drug manufacturers do not pay PDUFA fees for review of ANDAs. In 2002, the median approval time for original ANDAs was 18.2 months. At present, there are no statutory provisions for allowing generic biologics.

MEDICAL DEVICES

As we have seen, although there is a legal distinction between drugs and therapeutic biologics, there is far more commonality than difference both within and between the product groups, and with regard to the FDA approval process. The category of medical devices, by comparison, includes an incredible variety of instruments, machines, supplies, devices, reagents, software, and other substances (some of which are themselves biologics) that often seem to have little in common. Although the FDA recognizes about 1700 general categories of medical devices (which are grouped into 16 medical specialties known as panels, see Figure 4.3), there

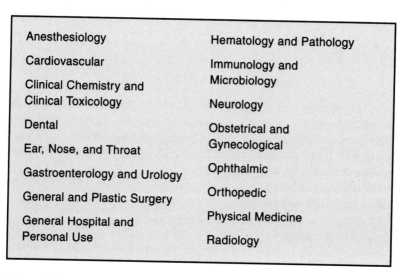

Anesthesiology	Hematology and Pathology
Cardiovascular	Immunology and Microbiology
Clinical Chemistry and Clinical Toxicology	Neurology
Dental	Obstetrical and Gynecological
Ear, Nose, and Throat	
Gastroenterology and Urology	Ophthalmic
General and Plastic Surgery	Orthopedic
General Hospital and Personal Use	Physical Medicine
	Radiology

Figure 4.3 Medical device classification panels.
Source: CDRH *Device Advice*

are thousands of products comprising iterations and combinations of these device types. More than 10,000 U.S. manufacturers of medical devices are listed by the CDRH. Not surprisingly, the regulation of medical devices is not at all straightforward.

Medical devices that were marketed before the Medical Device Amendments to the FD&C Act was signed into law in 1976 are referred to as preamendment devices. The amendments required all devices to be classified into one of three device classes, based on the extent of control necessary to provide reasonable assurance of safety and effectiveness. It took many years, but all preamendment devices have now been classified.

In general, medical device classification is related to the risk posed by the device. Class I devices present minimal potential for harm to the user and are often simpler in design than Class II or Class III devices. About 55 percent of medical devices are Class I, about 40 percent are Class II, and about five percent are Class III.[19]

Briefly, the classes of medical devices and the types of regulatory controls to which each class is subject are:

- Class I—General Controls
  - With exemptions
  - Without exemptions
- Class II—General Controls and Special Controls
  - With exemptions
  - Without exemptions
- Class III—General Controls and Premarket Approval

The lack of intuitive obviousness in device classification is apparent to the industry and, to some extent at least, to the FDA. A number of devices have been reclassified by CDRH, and many devices have been exempted from certain requirements. Generally, reclassification has moved devices from a higher to a lower class, but there are a few exceptions. The only way to be sure what's going on with class rank at a specific time is to check with the FDA.

General Controls

You will notice that general controls are requirements that apply to all devices in all three classes. As such, they can be considered as the minimum requirements for medical devices.

Unless specifically exempted by regulation, general controls, in essence, require device manufacturers to:

1. Register each manufacturing location.

2. List all marketed medical devices.

3. Manufacture devices in accordance with cGMP regulations.

4. Label devices in accordance with applicable regulations.

5. Submit a premarket notification [510(k)], unless the device is exempt from premarket notification or if it is identified as being subject to other requirements.

In recent years, most Class I devices and some Class II devices have been exempted from premarket notification and/or cGMP requirements. Up-to-date information from the FDA must be reviewed before a regulatory pathway for a new product is determined.

While general controls apply to all three classes of medical devices, they are the only level of controls that apply to Class I devices. Class I devices are subject to the least regulatory control because they present minimal potential for harm to the user and are often simpler in design than Class II or Class III devices.

Class I devices are *not* intended to be:

• For use in supporting or sustaining life;

• Of importance in preventing impairment to human life; and may not

• Present a potential unreasonable risk of illness or injury.

Examples of Class I devices are elastic bandages, dental burrs, tongue depressors, examination gloves, and the ever-popular enema kits. Most Class I devices are now exempt from the premarket notification and/or GMP regulation. However, the FDA believes that some Class I devices should remain subject to premarket notification requirements, that is, require 510(k) filing. Based on FDAMA provisions, a Class I device is exempt from the premarket notification requirements under section 510(k) of the act unless the device is intended for a use that is of substantial importance in preventing impairment of human health or it presents a potential unreasonable risk of illness or injury (referred to as "reserved criteria"). Based on these reserved criteria, the FDA has evaluated all Class I devices to determine which device types should be still subject to premarket notification requirements.[20] Examples of the so-called "reserved" Class I devices, which require premarket notification, are shown in Figure 4.4.

Ammonia test system

Bilirubin (total and unbound) in the neonate test system

Iron (non-heme) test system

Iron-binding capacity test system

Magnesium test system

Phosphorous (inorganic) test system

Testosterone test system

Uric acid test system

Antimony test system

Arsenic test system

Carbon monoxide test system

Cholinesterase test system

Mercury test system

Adenosine triphosphate release assay

Russell viper venom reagent

Blood bank supplies

Vacuum-assisted blood collection system

Transport culture medium

Microbiological specimen collection and transport device

Campylobacter fetus serological reagents

Chlamydia serological reagents

Epstein-Barr virus serological reagents

Mycobacterium tuberculosis immunofluorescent reagents

Trypanosoma spp. serological reagents

Dental handpiece and accessories

Boiling water sterilizer

Surgeon's glove

Pediatric position holder

Patient examination glove

Patient lubricant

Protective restraint

Ataxiagraph

Electroencephalogram (EEG) signal spectrum analyzer

Keratome

Goniometer

Mechanical wheelchair

Scintillation (gamma) camera

Positron camera

Figure 4.4   Examples of reserved Class I devices.

Source: Federal Register

About Premarket Notification. A few Class I and most Class II devices are cleared for commercial distribution or marketing through premarket notification. The main concept behind 510(k) clearance is the assumption that the device being reviewed by the FDA prior to its being marketed or distributed is substantially equivalent to one or more other devices already being sold in the United States. Specifically, the device must be regarded as substantially equivalent to a "predicate device," usually one marketed before the 1976 Medical Device Amendments (that is, a preamendment device); the predicate device can also be a postamendment device that has already been found to be substantially equivalent to a preamendment device. The FDA will find the new device equivalent if, after reviewing the submission, the FDA is convinced that:

- The device performs the same function and falls within an established type of predicate device.

- The technological characteristics of the new device are comparable to the predicate device.

- Whatever differences in characteristics that do exist between the new and predicate device will not raise any new safety and effectiveness questions.

Special Controls

Special controls apply to Class II medical devices. Class II devices are those for whom General Controls alone are not adequate to assure the safety and effectiveness of a device, based on the potential of risk to health posed by the device. Special Controls will vary from product to product, but may include special labeling requirements, conformance with certain FDA guidances, and mandatory performance standards, human clinical trials, and post-market surveillance.

Examples of Class II devices include powered wheelchairs, infusion pumps, and surgical drapes. A few Class II devices are exempt from the premarket notification requirement.

Premarket Approval

Premarket approval is the required process of scientific review to ensure the safety and effectiveness of most Class III devices, for which insufficient information exists to assure safety and effectiveness solely through general or special controls. An approved PMA application is, in effect, a private license granted to the applicant to market a particular medical device. It is similar in spirit to an NDA or BLA, and securing PMA approval for a new Class III medical device can sometimes be as rigorous as securing approval for a new pharmaceutical.

Class III devices are usually those that support or sustain human life, are of substantial importance in preventing impairment of human health, or that present a potential, unreasonable risk of illness or injury. Examples of Class III devices requiring a premarket approval include replacement heart valves, silicone gel–filled breast implants, and implanted cerebella stimulators. Based on certain complicated regulatory provisions, some Class III devices can be marketed with a premarket notification 510(k).

Class III devices generally need clinical evaluations, which are included in the PMA along with all other data involving safety, effectiveness, GMPs, and so on. PMA submissions are subjected to rigorous scientific review by both FDA personnel and an advisory committee representing the appropriate medical field. The requirements for PMA approval, like those for NDA and PLA approval, are very stringent.

Submissions to the FDA for 510(k)s and PMAs can range from relatively simple and straightforward to extremely complex. The FDA, of course, provides guidelines for preparing the required documents, but there is no boilerplate form.

The review of 510(k) submissions is supposed to be completed within 90 days, but that has rarely been the case. The mean total elapsed FDA review time for 510(k)s increased to 100 days in fiscal year 2002 from 96 in fiscal year 2001. The median review time for 510(k) submissions has decreased from a high of 164 days in fiscal year 1993 to 74 days in fiscal year 2002. The situation is more time-consuming for PMAs. The total elapsed time from PMA submission to decision in fiscal year 2001 was 411 days. In fiscal year 2002, the total elapsed time from submission to decision for PMAs had decreased to 364 days.[21] Considering that in the mid-1990s, the average elapsed time for PMAs hovered at about 800 days, considerable progress has been made.

The product group that comprises drugs, biologics, and medical devices is large, complicated, diverse, and often unwieldy. A key to successful medical product development is to thoroughly understand what is required by regulations for a particular new product, what is not required but likely to be expected or recommended by the FDA, and what is unnecessary or unwanted. Good rapport with the reviewing group at the FDA makes agreement on these issues much more likely. Really knowing your technology and product—how it is used, who will use it, what it does—and viewing the FDA as an overworked organization with enormous responsibility, rather than as an adversary, will make life easier and allow new products to be reviewed and approved more quickly.

5

Designing-In Quality

Almost all quality improvement comes via simplification of design, manufacturing, layout, processes, and procedures.

—Tom Peters

Once the toothpaste is out of the tube, it is awfully hard to get it back in.

—H. R. Haldeman

Volumes have been written about the value of TQM and focusing tools such as quality function deployment (QFD), which is a structured approach to defining customer needs or requirements and translating them into specific plans to produce products to meet those needs. In the arena of medical products, there is no debate. Applying quality principles to all company endeavors and deploying quality measures to ensure that customer requirements are coupled with product design are more than good ideas. They are requirements, and they are here to stay. Without documentation of the existence of quality processes and the verification that the processes are executed during product development, new healthcare products will not gain approval in the United States or be able to be sold in major overseas markets.

Medical product manufacturers are accustomed to establishing and following quality systems to help ensure that their products consistently meet specifications. Federal regulations specify that drugs and devices be manufactured in accordance with current good manufacturing practice (cGMP or GMP). GMP language is broad enough to describe minimum requirements for the methods, facilities, and controls used in the manufacturing, processing, packaging, and holding of products. GMP regulations for medical products do not prescribe in detail how a manufacturer must proceed as it designs and manufactures a specific product. Instead, a framework is presented requiring the manufacturer to develop and follow procedures and to fill in the appropriate details for a particular drug, biologic, or device. The upside of this umbrella approach is that it allows flexibility; the downside is that it can be vague enough to risk not getting it right (in the eyes of the FDA, that is). However, the most important philosophy behind GMPs is that *quality must be designed and built into a product.* If you're involved in medical product development, this must become a way of life.

Current GMP requirements now cover a full quality systems approach and should be regarded as quality system regulation. Indeed, device GMPs are known as quality system regulations (QSRs). The new terminology emphasizing quality is facilitating harmonization of FDA requirements with international standards. The FDA notes that the quality requirements—which also apply to product design and development—embodied in the revised regulations have been accepted worldwide as necessary to ensure that acceptable products are produced. This opinion is contested by some in industry who point out that certain FDA requirements, for example, in preclinical safety testing and in record-keeping requirements, may exceed those specified by international directives.

Historically, in the development of medical devices, the process of design has been regarded as taking on more significance than it does in the development of pharmaceuticals. Devices have special challenges with regard to materials selection, three-dimensional conformation, and such things as physical, mechanical, electrical, and chemical functionality. The SMDA of 1990 introduced a new element into medical device product development: it gave the FDA the authority to add preproduction design validation controls to the GMP regulations. While the resulting quality-focused design controls were crafted for medical devices, the principles and objectives of design controls are equally important to drugs, biologics, and obviously to combination products to make safe and effective products that conform to defined user needs and intended uses. By reviewing the design controls requirements for medical devices, the applicability and value of certain elements to other medical product categories should become clear.

The design phase is the most important development stage with regard to effect on the lifecycle of a device. It is at the design stage that the inherent safety, effectiveness, and reliability of a device are established. No matter how perfect a manufacturing process is, if the device doesn't have the qualities of safety, effectiveness, usability, and reliability designed into it, it isn't going to do what it's supposed to do the way it's supposed to do it. Only careful planning, review, and management of the processes involved in product development can assure that an acceptable product will be developed.

Design deficiencies are always costly and often dangerous. In an analysis of several years of medical device recalls, the FDA determined that about 40 percent were attributable to design defects. In some cases, the original product design was faulty, but was not detected until the product was in commercial use. In other cases, changes made to existing products—often in attempts to correct problems—produced new defects. Underscoring the significance of design is the unanimous 1996 ruling of the U.S. Supreme Court that consumers injured by certain medical devices because of faulty design can seek damages against the manufacturer under state law, even if the devices comply with FDA regulations.[22] The ruling applies to devices cleared through findings of substantial equivalence, although it has also been successfully applied to devices approved through the PMA process.

Once a project has passed through the design stage, it has a greater probability of becoming a new product. Typically, bad designs are likely to become bad products. It is difficult and costly to reverse the process before a product is launched, and even more difficult and costly to undo the damage in the marketplace after a poorly designed product is introduced. The costs associated with providing bad products can include internal failure costs (costs associated with defects found before the product makes it into the customers' hands); external failure costs (costs associated with defects found after the customer receives the product); appraisal costs (those incurred to determine quality issues leading to the problem); and prevention costs, to prevent a repeat occurrence.

Figure 5.1 illustrates the 1–10–100 rule, which summarizes the exponential relationship between the cost of correcting design defects and the stage of development.

The central philosophy of device GMPs as they affect product development is embraced in the concept of design controls.[23] In its essence, design controls constitute a system to ensure that a new product that is eventually manufactured can be used safely and effectively while meeting customer needs. What design controls require is for manufacturers to establish and maintain formal controls for their product development activities. There must be a process that takes product design through a series of steps, from identification of product requirements and specifications, through rigorous testing and validation. In other words, the seat-of-the-pants system of

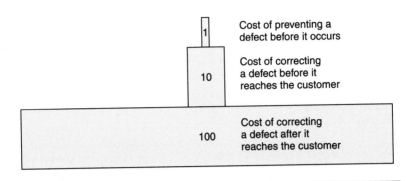

Figure 5.1   The 1–10–100 rule.

Source: Charles Gevirtz, *Developing New Products with TQM* (New York: McGraw-Hill, 1994): 8. Reproduced with permission of The McGraw-Hill Companies.

product development that had even recently been common in companies both large and small is gone for good.

A most significant challenge for anyone working in product development in the healthcare field, especially with medical devices where stringent controls and requirements are a relatively new issue, is overcoming a bad attitude. Having to do all of the things required by design controls is unfamiliar and unpleasant to many of the people involved in product development. Marketing people and scientists seem to be hit the hardest. Management also tends to be nonsupportive, unappreciative of the global impact of noncompliance, and is often critical of the perceived extra costs, delays, and human resource drains. In reality, there are still many medical device manufacturers that either knowingly or unwittingly ignore design controls.

There are a few optimistic and progressive manufacturers who actually regard design controls as an opportunity to improve their product development process. Far more, bridling at what they regard as yet another burden unjustifiably thrust upon them, continue to rant, resist, and protest. Others regard the new requirements as a necessary evil, and not unexpected in light of the evolving harmonization of international requirements for the marketing of medical devices. The point is that quality regulations are not going to go away, and those responsible for healthcare product development will have to lead the charge to keep up the momentum in their organizations.

Requirements for design controls are not intended to apply to the very early stages of product development, such as research, review of ideas, formulation of concepts, or preliminary feasibility studies. Once it is decided that a design will be developed, however, a plan must be put into effect that will establish the adequacy of the design requirements and that will ensure that the design that is eventually released to production meets all of the agreed-upon requirements.

Design controls implementation is required by the FDA for Class II and Class III devices, and for some Class I devices (see Figure 5.2), including those automated by computer software.

The regulations require each manufacturer to establish and maintain procedures for the following:

- Design and development planning

- Design input

- Design output

- Design review

- Design verification and validation

- Design transfer

- Design changes

- Design history file

A very stripped-down look at each element will help later to set the stage for creating an integrative product development process that will be compatible with the organization and structure of a device manufacturer, meet FDA requirements, facilitate securing permission to market internationally, and best of all, expedite the development of new, high-quality products.

Design and development planning requires that a plan be created to describe the activities that are necessary to design and develop the specific product and to define responsibility for its implementation. Interfaces among individuals, groups, and activities should be identified and

Catheter, tracheobronchial suction

Glove, surgeon's

Restraint, protective

System, applicator, radionuclide, manual

Source, radionuclide teletherapy

Devices automated with computer software

Figure 5.2   Class I devices subject to design controls.

described. For many new devices and associated manufacturing processes that use software, these tasks are further complicated because of the importance of software, and the possibility of subtle software errors. This stage is when clarity should be brought to the questions of: What is going to be done? Who is going to make sure it gets done? Who is going to do it? When will it all happen? Figure 5.3 indicates the kinds of items that might be included in a checklist for putting together a plan for design controls.

- User/patient requirements
- Physical characteristics and constraints of the device
- Regulatory and voluntary standards requirements
- Safety needs of the user
- Type of failure mode analysis
- Anticipated possible misuse of the device
- Elimination or minimization of user-related failures
- Need for fail-safe characteristics
- Producibility of the design
- Functional requirements
- Environmental requirements
- Test requirements: physical, chemical, biological, safety, efficacy
- Maximum and minimum tolerances
- Acceptance criteria
- Components selection
- Packaging requirements
- Sterilization method and requirements
- Labeling and instructions
- Shelf-life and storage requirements
- Serviceability and maintainability

Figure 5.3 Examples of items to include in a design controls checklist.

Design input includes all of the steps necessary to ensure that the design requirements for a specific device are appropriate for and address the intended use of the device, and meet the needs of both the user and the patient. In this stage, information is gathered about the performance requirements, and preliminary specifications for elements such as design characteristics, form and configuration, and materials are defined.

Design output is made up of the product and process documentation that is needed and used to transform a product idea into a prototype or finished product. It must also include the test plans, procedures, and reports that will verify that a product meets the design input requirements. The records and results of each design phase make up the design output. The nature and number of design phases is determined by the manufacturer.

Design review is a formal and documented procedure for assessing design results and is to be conducted at appropriate stages of the product development process. The design review is intended to ensure that the design of the product being developed conforms to the established criteria and to identify design deficiencies or defects. Reviews are supposed to be unbiased and objective examinations by appropriately trained individuals who do not have direct responsibility for design development. Thus, a key element for successful design review is the formal identification, designation, and utilization of independent participants. Design review should be conducted by representatives of all functions that have been involved with the design stage being reviewed. How frequently reviews are conducted is up to the manufacturer, reflecting the organization's staging of the product development process.

Design verification and validation refers to a series of ongoing procedures that ensure that a product's design output meets its design input and that the device conforms to defined user needs and intended uses. Generally, testing of prototype (or sometimes of production) units must take place both under defined test conditions and under actual or simulated use conditions. Preclinical and clinical testing, failure analysis, and cost analysis are part of the program.

Design transfer procedures ensure that the design basis for a device and its components is correctly translated into production specifications. It involves transferring all of the documentation from the design process to manufacturing. Of course, once the design is translated into physical form, the FDA specifies that its technical adequacy, safety, and reliability should be verified through comprehensive documented testing under simulated or actual use conditions.

Design changes do take place for various reasons. Each manufacturer must establish and maintain procedures for the identification, documentation, validation, verification, review, and approval of any design changes.

Design history file is the name given to the compendium of all the records, or reference to the records, that are necessary to demonstrate that the design of a specific product was developed in accordance with the approved design plan. For example, the results of all design reviews are included in the design history file.

The FDA is rather adamant that failure mode analysis be conducted at the beginning of the design effort and as part of each design review. The objective is to identify potential design weaknesses and inadequacies that might adversely affect safety and performance, and to then take corrective action to remove or minimize the undesirable effects. Failure mode analysis can be accomplished through fault tree analysis or through failure mode and effects criticality analysis. Details of these techniques, which are also addressed in chapter 6 of this book, are available from various sources.[24] The important thing is that a systematic way to identify and address potential design weaknesses be used and documented.

Manufacturers are free to develop and define the details of their own design control systems. They must, however, meet the general requirements of the GMP regulations. Everyone who works in medical product development must be committed to TQM, must be aware of the design control requirements in the FDA regulations, and must comply with the company's approved design control system to assure that the requirements are met. In fact, it should be the product development organization that creates the design control system.

6

Designing-Out Disaster: Risk Analysis

Haste in every business brings failures.

—Herodotus

As to diseases make a habit of two things—to help, or at least, to do no harm.

—Hippocrates

Try as one might, it is impossible to design and develop a product that is risk-free. Even if the best of all possible product development worlds could exist—in which a design is flawless, the labeling perfect, and clinical trial results unassailable—elements beyond the control of the most astute product development team will conspire to introduce the potential of product-related hazard. Have no doubt; someone or something will spoil the broth.

Risks can lead to hazards. A hazard is a potential source of harm, and medical products are associated with a dizzying array of hazards: biological hazards, chemical hazards, mechanical hazards, thermal hazards, electrical hazards, radiation hazards. There are hazards related to the use of a medical product, such as use in ways that are not anticipated by the manufacturer; use in ways that are anticipated, but are inadequately controlled; requirements for proper use that exceed the physical, perceptual, or cognitive abilities of the user; nonintuitive use, that is, inconsistent with a user's expectations; dependency of proper use on a specific environment, when the effect of environmental differences is not understood by the user or if proper use in specific environments exceeds the capacities of the user. Hazard is typically triggered by inherent risk of the product in medical treatment, product failure or malfunction, and the way the product is used. Sloppy, non-GMP manufacturing; undocumented and unreported changes made by suppliers of raw materials; inadequate quality control on the part of manufacturing equipment manufacturers; and slip-ups in the shipping, storage, and distribution chain are a just a few of the elements that can contribute to product hazard.

The challenges of reducing risk and hazard potential by making a product doctor-proof and patient-proof are well-known to most product developers. The truth is, regardless of whether a product has been demonstrated to be safe enough to gain FDA clearance or approval for marketing, there *will* be risk associated with its use.[25] In turn, "risk" is a relative term that has meaning only in the context of the benefit provided by the product. Risk and benefit, then, are subjective attributes, and at some point in product development, a call must be made whether the benefit of a medical product sufficiently outweighs the risk attendant to the product. Misjudgment of product risk and benefit further contribute to potential product hazard, the result of which can be harm to patients, product recalls, and product liability lawsuits. Major sources of medical product risks follow.

Product Defects

- Design defects
- Manufacturing defects
- Warning defects

Side Effects

- Avoidable known side effects: predictable reactions under certain, improper conditions of use (usually clarified by product labeling)
- Unavoidable known side effects: inherent physical or physiologic reactions that can be expected to occur even with proper product use
- Unknown side effects/consequences:
  - Associated with long-term use

- Associated with concurrent use of other products

- Associated with off-label (unapproved or unstudied) uses

- Associated with use in an unstudied patient population

Use Errors

- By healthcare professional

- By patient

- By caregiver

Potential interactions of these contributing risk elements to cause harm are shown in Figure 6.1.

Risk assessment is the process of identifying, estimating, and evaluating the nature and severity of risks associated with a product. It is an important component of design controls, and is a process that should take place throughout a product's lifecycle. To avoid problems during the later stages of product development or after product launch, it is important to have as good an idea as possible of the product's underlying risks and benefits prior to FDA approval or clearance for marketing.

Those involved in product development planning play a key role in providing the greatest possible assurance that the risk of a new product is as minimal as can be. They also should play a critical role in determining the extent to which the product's benefits are expected to outweigh its risks.

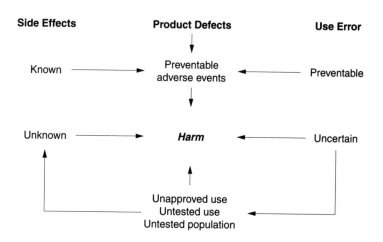

Figure 6.1   Examples of risk.

If for some reason upper management does not recognize either the ethical or business implications of minimizing risk, the personal liability they may face should a product prove to be hazardous for reasons that were identifiable and/or avoidable might get their attention.

While a product development team may have a vanishingly small or nonexistent role in the manufacturing, prescribing, dispensing, and ultimate use of a healthcare product, it does have considerable influence over design control, development, testing, and labeling of a new medical device, biologic, or drug. Indeed, prudent pharmaceutical companies have begun to incorporate risk reduction activities during the drug development phase.[26]

Instituting a system for risk management as part of the product development process will facilitate understanding and addressing the factors relevant to the potential of a product to cause harm. This process can be tailored to the specific category and use of the new product, but at the very least should provide the means to accomplish the objectives shown in Figure 6.2.

Medical device manufacturers are more familiar with traditional methods of risk analysis because the FDA's quality system regulation for medical devices requires risk analysis, where appropriate—that is, unless the manufacturer can document justification to the contrary. Since being an

1. *Identify* the potential sources of risk in the product and with reasonably anticipated use of the product.

2. *Describe* how hazardous use situations occur.

3. *Analyze* the causes for identified failure modes and risk sources.

4. *Evaluate* the seriousness of risk and the severity of potential harm.

5. *Eliminate, correct, minimize, or accept* the defects or weaknesses by redesigning, reformulating, labeling, and so on.

6. *Reevaluate* risk/benefit based on the above.

7. *Document* the processes and findings.

8. *Communicate* findings and recommendations to other decision makers.

Figure 6.2 Objectives of risk assessment and management.

apologist is in itself risky, in reality risk analysis is a must for a manufacturer to be able to make an ethical and business call on whether a new device is safe enough to market.[27] Although not expressly required for FDA approval for drugs and biologics, the principles of risk analysis techniques are applicable to these products, and are key elements in risk management strategies for drugs and biologics, as well as for medical devices. A variety of failure mode analyses are used to determine malfunctions, or signs of malfunctioning, that appear either immediately before or immediately after the failure of a critical parameter in a product or system. These analysis methods, in various ways, identify:

- Accident scenarios: What could/did go wrong, and what is the probability of occurrence?

- Consequence scenarios: What are the possible outcomes, and how serious are they?

FAILURE MODE ANALYSIS

Failure mode analysis determines which malfunction symptoms appear immediately before or after a failure of a critical parameter in a system. After all the possible causes are listed for each symptom, the product is designed to eliminate the problems. Failure mode and effects analysis (FMEA) identifies potential design inadequacies that may adversely affect safety and performance. Each potential failure mode, including possible human-induced failures or unusual hazardous situations, is considered in light of its probability of occurrence. In the case of medical devices, two techniques are typically (but not exclusively) used: fault tree analysis (FTA), and failure mode and effects criticality analysis (FMECA).[28] Grossly simplified, FTA asks, "What happened?" and provides the most likely answers, while FMECA asks, "What could happen?" and provides the most likely answers.

Fault Tree Analysis

Fault tree analysis (FTA) represents a deductive approach to failure mode analysis. It begins by assuming that a failure or safety hazard has occurred (for example, my printer doesn't work), and works backward to identify the defects, conditions, interactions, and so on, that could lead to the failure (for example, the printer is not plugged in, the printer cable is damaged, the proper driver is not installed). As a top-down approach, FTA is especially applicable to analysis of after-the-fact problems, when an unwanted event has already occurred.

Failure Mode and Effects Criticality Analysis

Failure mode and effects criticality analysis (FMECA) is an inductive process that begins by identifying and assuming defects at a basic component level (for example, the printer is not plugged in, the printer cable is damaged, the proper driver is not installed) and then determines the effects on higher system levels (for example, the printer won't work). As a bottoms-up approach that anticipates what could go wrong, FMECA is especially useful during the design and development stages of products. FMECA should be iterative to correspond with the nature of the specific design process.[29]

In addition to identifying potential failure modes, FMECA assigns a value to the severity of the effect and to how important the failure is to the safety of the device (criticality). A qualitative but numeric value is also assigned to the probability of occurrence of each identified failure mode. Often, a lower score is assigned to a higher degree of risk or probability. That is, if a failure mode can be expected to occur frequently, it might be assigned a value of 1, while a failure mode with a remote likelihood of occurrence might be given a 20. Ditto for the scoring of the seriousness or severity of the outcome of a failure event. This approach seems counterintuitive, and therefore subject to misinterpretation and misuse by all but seasoned risk analyzers. A more analyst-friendly approach is to assign a high number to a high likelihood of failure, and a low number to a low likelihood of failure, and a high number to a severe effect, and a low number to a mild effect.

There is no purpose in conducting risk analysis during product development or technology assessment if no one is able or willing to make the call on whether a product is safe enough. Just as the exact format for FMECA can be customized to specific products, so must the definition and assignment of criticality factors and decision-making criteria be customized. For example a risk score of 10 derived from some arbitrary FMECA protocol matrix may be absolutely unacceptable for a cardiovascular stent, but might be a good score for an artificial heart. The risk–benefit relationship has to be folded into the mix. So FMECA is simultaneously qualitative and quantitative, objective and subjective. Never back-fit a product into the matrix to obtain an acceptable score. A generic example of an FMECA scoring matrix is shown in Table 6.1.

When corners are cut in the identification, analysis, and minimization of risk, the cost can be adverse events, product recalls, and product liability litigation. Adapting and applying failure mode analysis methods to the product development planning process for all new medical products—whether the products are being developed internally or acquired from an external source—will enhance the quality techniques that lead to safe and effective medical devices, drugs, and biologics.

Table 6.1   Example of FMECA matrix.

Component or Function	Failure Mode	Effect Caused by Failure	Probability of Failure[1]	Severity of Effect[2]	Criticality Score[3]	User Detection Means	Corrective Action/ Applicable Controls

[1] Probability of occurrence of failure:
   Remote = 1
   Unlikely = 2
   Occasional = 3
   Frequent = 4

[2] Severity of effect of failure
   Minor (no injury; product function not affected) = 1
   Moderate (temporary illness or injury or product failure) = 4
   Major (injury or illness requiring intervention; definite product failure) = 7
   Critical (permanent injury or illness, requiring extensive intervention) = 10
   Catastrophic (death or major permanent disability) = 15

[3] Probability × Severity

7

Recalls, Revocations, and Withdrawals

There are some things that are sure to go wrong as soon as they stop going right.

—Celia Elizabeth Green

It isn't that they can't see the solution. It is that they can't see the problem.

—G.K. Chesterton

For medical products manufacturers, the cost of compliance with FDA regulations is high. Strict adherence to the principles of good product development, good clinical practices, good manufacturing practices, post-marketing surveillance, and other must-do tasks requires time, money, and effective human effort. The price, though, represents a sound investment, considering that the cost of noncompliance can quickly eclipse the cost of compliance. For reasons that may be unintentional or intentional, unforeseeable or readily foreseen, products sometimes don't meet standards and expectations related to such considerations as manufacturing, performance, or safety—which can lead to a temporary or permanent removal of the product from the marketplace. In mid-2003, the FDA announced that it would be stepping up enforcement actions, including removing products from the market.[30]

RECALLS

A recall is a firm's removal or correction of a marketed product, including its labeling and/or promotional materials, that the FDA considers to be in violation of the laws it administers, and against which the agency could initiate legal action (for example, seizure or the full range of administrative and civil actions available to the agency). A product recall is not a remedial action; it is the cost of failure, which is frequently the consequence of noncompliance. Product recalls can be voluntary (initiated by the company); semi-voluntary (at the suggestion of the FDA, with acquiescence of the manufacturer); or statutory (a result of the FDA obtaining a court order authorizing U.S. marshals to seize the product because the manufacturer refuses to see the light). The FDA classifies recalls into one of three classes to indicate the relative degree of health hazard presented by the product being recalled[31]:

- Class I is a situation in which there is a reasonable probability (strong likelihood) that the use of, or exposure to, a violative product will cause serious adverse health consequences or death.

- Class II is a situation in which the use of, or exposure to, a violative product may cause temporary or medically reversible adverse health consequences or where the probability of serious adverse health consequences is remote.

- Class III is a situation in which the use of, or exposure to, a violative product is not likely to cause adverse health consequences.

Many less-serious voluntary recalls involve only specific lots, batches, or manufacturing runs, and the manufacturer can continue to market the product except for the specifically recalled examples. Such recalls often involve out-of-specification product resulting from temporary and solvable problems in manufacturing, storage, or shipment. The recalled products are usually destroyed, but in some cases they can be reconditioned to comply with FDA regulations. Manufacturers usually carry out their responsibilities to protect the public health by voluntarily recalling products that are defective or present a risk of injury to consumers.

MARKET WITHDRAWALS

A market withdrawal is a manufacturer's removal or correction of a distributed product for either a minor violation for which the FDA would not normally initiate legal action, or for certain reasons that do not involve a violation at all (for example, normal stock rotation practices, routine equipment adjustments and repairs, product improvements). The removal of medical products from the market as a result of actual or alleged tampering is also considered a market withdrawal, even in the absence of manufacturing or distribution problems. A *safety-based withdrawal*, however, is a complete cessation of the marketing of a drug because of an intrinsic property of the drug that poses serious safety concerns.

REVOCATIONS

A revocation is the cancellation of a license of a biological product and of the authorization to ship a biological product for sale, barter, or exchange in interstate commerce. A revocation may occur either at the request of the manufacturer, or when grounds exist for the FDA to initiate such an action.

The removal of products by recall, withdrawal, or revocation almost always applies to products that have already been cleared or approved for marketing and have already been launched to the market. As someone involved in product development planning, and not involved with manufacturing or marketing, you might think that you're off the hook with regard to recalls, withdrawals, and revocations. Not so. While some market removals result from completely unpredictable causes (for example, consumer tampering of a drug or device) or the appearance of new diseases that could affect the safety of source materials for certain biologics (for example, blood donors who later develop variant Creutzfeldt-Jakob disease), most do not.

From 1975–1999, 548 new drugs were approved, and 16 (2.9 percent) were withdrawn from the market.[32] In 2001, 240 prescription drugs were recalled, and two drugs were withdrawn from the market for safety reasons.[33] Although it may take years for the adverse effects of a new drug to be observed, this is not always the case, as can be seen in Table 7.1.

Device companies have historically been less compliant with FDA regulations than drug companies, and the incidence of device recalls, as a percentage of products marketed, is greater than the incidence of drug recalls (see Figures 7.1 and 7.2).[34] Biologics products account for the greatest number of recall actions (see Figure 7.3).

INFLUENCE OF PRODUCT DEVELOPMENT PLANNING

There are measures that can be taken during product development planning that can reduce the likelihood of a product becoming the subject of a recall.

Table 7.1 Recent safety-based drug withdrawals.

Drug Trade Name	Use	Year Approved	Year Withdrawn
Baycol	Cholesterol lowering	1997	2001
Raplon	Injectable anesthesia/ muscle relaxant	1999	2001
Latronex	Irritable bowel syndrome treatment	2000	2000
Propulsid	Nighttime heartburn treatment	1993	2000
Rezulin	Type 2 diabetes treatment	1997	2000
Hismanal	Antihistamine	1988	1999
Raxar	Antibiotic	1997	1999
Posicor	Hypertension, stable angina treatment	1997	1998
Duracet	Pain reliever	1997	1998
Seldane, Seldane-D	Antihistamine	1985	1998
Pondimin	Obesity treatment	1973	1997
Redux	Obesity treatment	1996	1997

Source: Food and Drug Administration, Center for Drug Evaluation and Research, "Safety-Based Drug Withdrawals" (1997–2001)

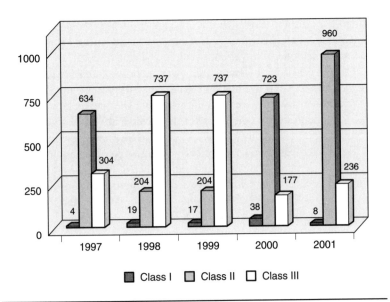

Figure 7.1 CDRH five-year recall statistics.
Source: CDRH

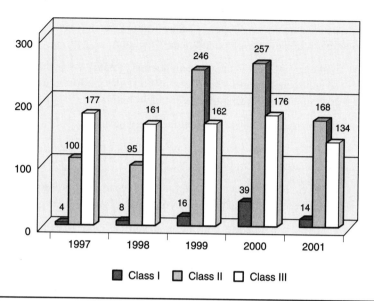

Figure 7.2   CDER five-year recall statistics.
Source: CDER

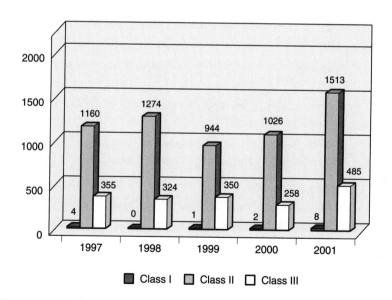

Figure 7.3   CBER five-year recall statistics.
Source: CBER

Important questions that should be addressed and readdressed during new product planning and development phases include:

- Is there confidence that the manufacturing entity—whether internal or contracted—can and will manufacture the product consistently and reliably according to cGMP requirements?

- Is the product's target population clearly defined?

- Does the product carry a high probability of being used outside of the target patient population?

  - If yes, is there a reasonably foreseeable safety risk associated with the use of the product in other groups?

  - If yes, can labeling, education, and surveillance reduce the risk?

- Have clinical trials adequately examined the safety and efficacy of the product in a reasonably representative target population?

- Is the product designed so that its intended use is intuitive?

  - If no, can labeling and education clearly describe intended use?

- Is the product designed so that its application or administration is intuitive?

  - If no, can labeling and education clearly and effectively convey instructions?

- Is the safety profile of each individual component or ingredient of the product known?

- Is there previous knowledge of the interactions of the component materials or ingredients?

- Have the principles and requirements of design controls been implemented for products that are medical devices?

- Has a rigorous risk analysis been conducted to identify and quantify the hazards of product failure and product misuse?

No one can make a product that is foolproof or that will be safe and effective for each and every patient who will ever be exposed to the product. Keeping the patients and the users of the products foremost in mind during development or acquisition of a new product will bring one a little closer to that unattainable goal.

8

Human Factors and the Nature of Relationships
Minimizing Medical Errors

Four legs good, two legs bad.

—George Orwell

Be careful about reading health books. You may die of a misprint.

—Mark Twain

It is highly likely that at some time in your life you have encountered a product that you regarded as difficult, if not impossible, to use. Perhaps the problem related to a package that defied opening, or a difficult-to-read label that didn't provide the information needed. Perhaps the product was awkward to maneuver, or its regular use resulted in a repetitive stress injury. Such encounters often lead to dissatisfaction with a product or even to misuse of a product.

When the paths of a human being and some healthcare technology cross, an extensive array of critical interactions takes place. These interactions occur whether the technology involves a product that falls into the category of drug, biologic, or medical device; and these interactions occur regardless of whether the human is the individual purchasing the product, using the product, or upon whom the product is used. The discipline that seeks to analyze and optimize the relationship between human being and any technology is known as *human factors*.

In recent years, the FDA has exhibited a growing interest in human factors. The driving force in this interest was the realization by the agency that use-error is a significant cause of patient morbidity and mortality. The FDA now wants manufacturers of medical devices to pay attention to human factors early in the product development process to catch and correct problems related to interfaces before a healthcare product reaches the market.[35] For example, the FDA expects human factors studies to be encompassed in the user-interface design and validation activities of the design controls requirements included in the current revised QSRs (that is, GMPs) for medical devices (Figure 8.1 summarizes the CDRH definition and benefits of human factors in medical device design). In other words, a device manufacturer will be required to document that human factors were considered in the process of design development.[36] To assist industry in fulfilling this requirement, the FDA has formed a human factors engineering team at CDRH, and has issued a number of publications relating to human factors. These documents (see Figure 8.2) are very helpful in explaining the objective of human factors engineering and the importance of incorporating human factors into medical device design. The FDA has also expressed an interest in applying human factors principles to the labeling of drugs and biologics, as well as devices. Unfortunately, by stressing the role of human factors in product development of devices, and in focusing on labeling-related human error issues for drugs and biologics, the FDA is itself guilty of major human factors violations in failing to take into account the following:

• Design issues are not exclusive to devices, but apply to drugs, biologics, and combination products. They all have shapes, sizes, colors, means of deployment or administration, instructions for use, susceptibility to confusion with other products, and so on.

• All medical products must in some way accommodate the characteristics of the users and of the environments in which the products are used. By definition, then, human factors come into play.

• The FDA's labeling issues have been reactive to error. For example, by the time prescribing and dispensing errors had occurred because the drug trade names Celebrex (anti-inflammatory), Celexa (antidepressant), and Cerebyx (antiseizure) all look and sound similar, harm had already occurred.

• There is too much FDA focus on individual errors, as opposed to system errors. A pharmacist misreading a sloppily written prescription for Celexa and dispensing Celebrex constitutes individual error; inadequate means of generating prescriptions or of implementing patient records might be system errors contributing to that individual error. In early 2003 there

"Human factors (HF) is the study of how people use technology. It involves the interaction of human abilities, expectations, and limitations, with work environments and system design.

The term "human factors engineering" (HFE) refers to the application of human factors principles to the design of devices and systems. It is often interchanged with the terms "human engineering," "usability engineering," or "ergonomics."

The goal of HFE is to design devices that users accept willingly and operate safely in realistic conditions. In medical applications, HFE helps improve human performance and reduce the risks associated with use error.

In many cases, HFE focuses on the device user interface (also called the UI or the man-machine interface). The user interface includes all components and accessories necessary to operate and properly maintain the device, including the controls, displays, software, logic of operation, labels, and instructions.

Specific benefits of HFE include:

- Reduced risk of device use error;
- Better understanding of device status and operation;
- Better understanding of a patient's current medical condition;
- Easier to use (or more intuitive) devices;
- Reduced need for training;
- Reduced reliance on user manuals;
- Easier to read controls and displays;
- Safer connections between devices (i.e. power cords, leads, tubes, etc.);
- More effective alarms; and
- Easier repair and maintenance.

HFE should take place early in the product development process. It should include tools such as analysis of critical tasks, use error hazard and risk analysis, and realistic use testing."

Figure 8.1 CDRH comments on human factors.

Source: CDRH, *Human Factors Engineering Group Brochure*

Document Title

- Overview of FDA's New Human Factors Program Plan: Implications for the Medical Device Industry

- Do It by Design: An Introduction to Human Factors in Medical Devices

- Write It Right: Recommendations for Developing User Instruction Manuals for Medical Devices Used in Home Health Care

- Human Factors General Information

- Human Factors and the FDA's Goals: Improved Medical Device Design

- Human Factors Implications of the New GMP Rule

- Human Factors Points to Consider for IDE Devices

- Human Factors and Postmarket Surveillance at FDA

- CDRH's Approach to Providing Human Factors Information

All of the above documents are available online from CDRH.

Figure 8.2   Examples of FDA publications on the topic of human factors.

was a tragic and well-publicized case in which a human heart of an incompatible tissue type was transplanted into a young girl, who later died. There were systems in place to prevent such an occurrence, yet the systems were inadequate and failed to prevent individual error.

   • The FDA itself has reported that of the medication errors that occurred during May 2001, 42 percent were attributed to human factors. As can be seen from Table 8.1, the other categories of error were communication, name confusion, labeling, and packaging/design—all of which entail human factors issues. One can only marvel at the failure of the agency to recognize this.

   Medical errors occur when a medical product is used incorrectly, or when there is a failure to use the product as intended. Medical products can harm patients, family members, or healthcare providers. The potential harm arises primarily from two sources:

   1. Failure of the product

   2. Actions of the user

Table 8.1 Medication errors by cause during May 2001.

Causes	Number	% of Total
Communication	64	19%
Name confusion	44	13%
Labeling	68	20%
Packaging/design	20	6%
Human factors	145	42%

Source: FDA Center for Drug Evaluation and Research, *Drug Safety Page* (1 October 2001)

Hazards associated with drugs, devices, and biologics are a serious problem. An Institute of Medicine report estimated that in U.S. hospitals, between 44,000 and 98,000 people die each year from medical errors. This is more than the number who die yearly from motor vehicle accidents, breast cancer, or AIDS.[37] Safer medical products can reduce the incidence and consequences of medical errors. Attention to human factors in product design can minimize the likelihood of both product failure and product misuse.

It also makes obvious good business sense to take human factors seriously in the design of all new FDA-regulated healthcare products. Good products sell well; bad products can lead to lawsuits.

It is important to recognize that people interface with products on a variety of levels, including those that are physical, perceptual or sensory, and cognitive. While no single product presentation can be ideal for all customers or users, there are areas of primary concern that can be addressed and optimized to mesh with the corporeal, psychological, and intellectual limits of the majority of customers or users.

Ergonomics is the science that deals with the dimensional and physical interfaces between humans and products. Something as fundamental as anatomical fit is surprisingly often overlooked in medical product development. For example, some medical devices can't be manipulated comfortably or accurately because the portions of the device required for its control are simply too large to fit in a user's hand. Average or small women, or smaller than average men might have this type of problem. Indeed, the majority of men or women in some ethnic groups might not be able to use such a device appropriately. The demographics of the workplace and workers must be known and accommodated to ensure that such things as size and strength of the product users are not impediments to safe and efficacious use of those products. On occasion, the FDA has refused approval for a device because the clinical trials did not show that users could successfully use the device.

The patient, too, must be considered in human factors analyses. Small babies cannot be given tablets; very elderly patients or disabled individuals may have extreme difficulty using pharmaceuticals in certain forms of administration or packaging. Devices that must conform to some part of a patient's body clearly need this type of assessment. Electrodes, cuffs, dressings, intravenous catheters, urinary catheters, flexible endoscopes, and surgical implants are obvious examples of devices that require differing sizes and conformations depending on whether used in neonatal, pediatric, or adult patients. Similarly, any product that is expected to be used directly by a patient must be suitable for such things as the strength, gender, dexterity, handedness, educational level, physical maturity, and functional capability of the patient.

Cognitive factors come into play in the intellectual relationship between humans and products. Is the method of handling and operation intuitive? If not, is it sufficiently easy to determine or learn how to use a product? Is the labeling informative and legible? With medical products, there can be no tolerance for ambiguity. The end user—whether physician, nurse, patient, or other—must understand how, when, why, where, and how often a drug, biologic, or device is to be used.

Sometimes cognitive elements are forgotten in the search for cosmetic appeal. Consider the black-on-black finish and labeling on some electronic equipment such as VCRs and compact disc players. These components are very attractive, but require something short of floodlights, five minutes, and a six-inch focal point to find the right push buttons. It's one thing to mistakenly press *rewind* rather than *play* on a tape deck. It's quite another thing to mistakenly press the wrong button on a diagnostic device because the requirements for lighting are in excess of the lighting normally available in use conditions.

This is not to say that appearances can be ignored. People do interact with products on a sensory or perceptual level, too. The style, shape, or color of a product can elicit an emotional response. If that response is negative, a negative attitude is likely to be transferred to the product whether or not that product is safe, effective, and meets a market need. Medical products, especially, need to be presented in a manner that suggests quality and care. Product appearance and presentation and the reaction to appearance and presentation can have a significant effect on the purchaser (or influencer) and user.

As has already been emphasized, cGMP requirements for medical devices call for manufacturers to ensure that a device will perform to meet both its intended use and the needs of the user. Applying human factors principles to product design will minimize the potential for use error and for the patient injuries that come from use error. The FDA suggests conducting appropriate human factors studies, analyses, and tests from the early stages of design until the point of interface of the product with the user and the patient is fixed. There are a number of ways to obtain the human factors data that relate to the FDA requirements. It is wise to examine the human factors that relate to business and market advantage requirements at the same time.

In terms of human factors analysis, the goals of those involved in product development should be to:

- Know the customer.

- Listen to the customer.

- Observe the customer.

- Act as the customer.

Customer is used loosely to include purchaser, influencer, and user.

The cardinal rule relating to person–product interfaces in healthcare product development is: know the users and the customers. Very basically, then, the first steps in a human factors analysis might very well include the identification exercises shown in Figure 8.3. With any given medical product, the relative importance of each question will vary, as will the relative complexity.

- Identify the customer. Who is the purchaser or who influences purchase?

- Identify the user. Who will be the hands-on user of the product? Is the user the customer?

- Identify the capabilities and limitations of the user. What are the characteristics of the physical and mental abilities of the user?

- Identify the subject. Who are the patients or individuals upon whom the product is being used?

- Identify the workplace. What is the environment in which the product will be used, and what are the limitations of the environment (for example, space, light, temperature)?

- Identify the utility. What is the purpose of the product and what are the clinical, market, and user needs it fills?

Figure 8.3 Examples of general questions relative to demography and products.

Within each of these identification tasks, there will be a number of subsets of activities. For example, consider the issue of identifying the hands-on user and obtaining critical demographic information. Suppose that it is determined that the user fits within the general category known as *nurse*. Additional data gathering about the user profile might well address the following:

- Are the users likely to be specialists?

- Which specialties are represented by users?

- What is the level of training, education, and experience of the users?

- What is the typical ratio of male to female users?

- What are the relevant anthropometric data for the users?

- Is the size, format, configuration, labeling, packaging, and so on, of the product compatible with the users?

- Are there cross-cultural issues?

Once the user is identified, it is important to define and understand what the user needs are, in terms of product function and performance. Once needs are understood, user expectations are determined—that is, what the user would want in terms of the product attributes. These attributes may often include the "bells and whistles." Remember, it may not be possible to fulfill all user expectations in a product, so it is necessary to identify the combination of product characteristics discernible to the user that represent the most important product characteristics. The goals of the product design should be a match between user expectations, technological feasibility, and cost considerations. Customer feedback on positive and negative attributes of existing products and about identified or anticipated needs that are not met by existing products is extremely important. It is important to listen carefully to what customers say, predict, gripe about, and praise in terms of your products, your competitors' products, prototypes, and product concepts. Don't fall into the trap of thinking that you know more than the customers.

One particularly effective method of obtaining information about customers, users, patients, procedures, current products, and environments is through directly observed customer behavior.[38] While techniques such as focus groups, one-on-one interviews, and surveys have value, they rely on opinions and self-reported behavior, which may not be accurate; furthermore, they cannot reflect unarticulated user needs. Direct observation, on the other hand, can provide a wealth of information that simply cannot be derived from questionnaires or roundtable discussions. Direct observation of diagnostic, therapeutic, surgical, and other relevant procedures is best done by a small cross-functional group. Someone skilled in human factors analysis will see problems, solutions, and opportunities that differ from those seen by a product development scientist or a marketing specialist. Thus, in addition to data critical to the development of the envisioned new product, the observation exercises may very well lead to ideas for entirely different new product opportunities.

Beyond observation, the greatest degree of empathy and identification with the customer is actually to act as the customer would act, to whatever extent possible. This entails putting oneself into the place of the customer (or user) in a real use or simulated setting. If a medical device can be manipulated and deployed without direct involvement with or compromise to a patient, those in a product development organization should make every effort to manipulate and deploy existing products and product prototypes in actual use situations. If the opportunity for this exercise is not possible in a clinical setting because of possible risk to patients, personnel, equipment, or so forth, role-playing in simulated situations is possible. Using products and prototypes in preclinical operative or therapeutic procedures, using anatomical models, and creating mock scenarios all allow one to put one-self into something approximating the role of the customer in terms of assessing human factors and product design.

If, following human factors analysis, it is determined that a new product concept or new product—in its entirety—is not fully compatible with its potential users, a business decision will have to balance the trade-offs among alternatives. Should the product be redesigned to increase its accept-ability to the users? Should multiple versions or sizes be made available? Or is the risk of nonuse or misuse of the product because of its human factors limitations acceptable to the company from both a potential product liability perspective and a reduced market share perspective? Market need, of course, must be clearly identified or firmly created. The element of util-ity is extremely important to human factors consideration. It is clearly a waste of time, money, and energy to develop a healthcare product that cannot be matched to an identified customer or market need.

One issue affecting human factors assessment is the drive toward design and development of a new healthcare product for worldwide mar-kets. The globalization trend in product development is likely to be met with unanticipated product launch flops if human factors are not carefully considered. In addition to the more obvious factors such as size differ-ences among some populations, there are cognitive factors that can have a significant impact on the acceptability of a product. Background, edu-cation, and training of the product users in some third-world countries, for example, may differ substantially from those of users in the United States. These differences, in turn, may necessitate major design or labeling modifications to assure use of a product at all, much less safe and effective use of the product.

Cultural biases involving diagnostic and therapeutic procedures can work against a successful global development and launch of a new product, as can differences in attitudes toward the significance of particular symptoms. There has been a history of preference for certain types of procedures and therapies, as well as a reluctance to engage in other practices, associated with particular countries. These opinions will affect the perceived clinical utility of a given healthcare product. It is important not to overlook these culturally related human factors if a new product is to be introduced into markets in different cultures or into multicultural markets.

Applying human factors principles to product development will allow an integration of user/customer requirements, user/customer expectations, clinical utility, marketing needs, and cost considerations into product design. Product development requires designing a relationship between technology and people.

9

Is It Safe and Does It Work?

Evaluating Safety and Efficacy in Clinical Trials

Test everything. Keep what is good.

—I Thessalonians 5:21

Never say, "I tried it once and it did not work."

—Lord Ernest Rutherford

Before a medical product can be marketed in the United States, the FDA must be given reasonable confidence that the product will be safe and effective when it is used. For most new drugs, biologics, Class III devices, and some Class II devices, reasonable confidence comes by way of clinical trials—that is, studies in humans. Clinical trial failures claim a great financial toll on the medical products industry. Failures occur when a company terminates a study because the product is not effective, or, worse, causes unexpected harm; or when the completed trials fail to satisfy FDA requirements for adequate and rigorous demonstration of safety and efficacy. It is never possible to guarantee the results of a clinical trial, or there would be no need for such trials in the first place. So planning and execution are especially important.

Before a drug, biologic, or device can be tested in humans, however, there must be compelling evidence that the product is safe enough to test in people. To establish that a medical product is reasonably safe, new products being developed are subjected to a variety of laboratory and animal tests.

PRECLINICAL TESTING

Preclinical (or nonclinical) testing refers to evaluations of both safety and efficacy in *in vitro*, *ex vivo*, or *in vivo* systems other than in human beings. Although the principal purpose of preclinical testing is to provide evidence of safety and performance before involving human subjects, in some instances the testing may suffice in lieu of testing in humans. For example, some medical products for which it would be unethical or not feasible to conduct clinical trials may be approved by the FDA based on animal studies.[39] It is estimated that only five in 5000 pharmaceuticals that enter preclinical testing advance to human trials, and that of these five, only one will eventually be marketed as a new product.[40]

Odds are generally much better for medical devices. By definition, devices do not involve metabolic processes for their primary effect. In contrast to the drug development process, development of medical devices does not usually involve screening enormous numbers of candidate technologies. Furthermore, it is usually easier to design safety and efficacy into a device using principles of mechanics and human factors than it is to design safety and efficacy into a pharmaceutical through molecular modeling. All of this means that many device types can be extensively and accurately evaluated in mechanical or anatomical models and in chemical, biological, and physical laboratory test procedures. Simulated-use testing of prototype designs can quickly weed out devices not likely to succeed before animals need to be involved. Implantable and absorbable medical devices, however, are more similar to drugs in their testing requirements, since properties such as long-term effects, metabolic fate, excretion, and storage profiles often must be examined. Nevertheless, the chemical and biological evaluations of pharmaceuticals and devices involve differing experimental approaches.

The FDA has guidelines and regulations regarding the type of data and results it expects to see for pharmaceuticals before considering testing on humans, but the agency generally does not tell drug companies what specific laboratory evaluations or animal tests to run. It is important, however, to ensure the quality and reliability of preclinical safety studies. This is normally accomplished through the conduct of the studies in compliance with good laboratory practice (GLP) regulations, which emphasize quality and ethics. To this end, the agency offers guidelines dealing with GLPs, which outline the requirements for quality assurance.[41] GLPs essentially impose the use of quality standards covering a number of elements of preclinical testing, particularly:

- Organization and personnel

- Facilities

- Equipment

- Testing facilities operation

- Test materials and control materials

- Protocols

- Record keeping and reports

In vivo or in vitro nonclinical laboratory studies to provide safety data in support of marketing applications for drugs, biologics, and medical devices must be done according to GLP. Certain other studies—for example, screening, dose-ranging, and preliminary efficacy studies—are exempt from GLP requirements. One caveat for product developers is that the universities with whom many contract for conduct of preclinical studies frequently do not comply with GLP requirements. Laboratory choice is important.

The nature of the drug (and of many biologics) being tested and the clinical test plans give scope and definition to the specific preclinical protocols and studies that are required to demonstrate safety and efficacy. Occasionally, customary animal models may be inappropriate or unsuited to a new product being tested. In this case, the test sponsors are encouraged to discuss testing approaches with the FDA.

Biological evaluations of medical devices to determine the potential toxicity resulting from contact of the device materials with the body are typically more defined than they are for drug or biologics. Testing is designed to determine that the device materials: (1) do not produce adverse local or systemic effects; (2) are not carcinogenic; and (3) do not cause adverse reproductive or developmental effects. In 1995, the FDA agreed to replace its existing guidance on biocompatibility with ISO 10993 Part 1: "Biological Evaluation of Medical Devices," with some modifications added to areas where the FDA did not regard the international guidance as having adequate rigor.[42] Tables 9.1 and 9.2 show the harmonized test matrices.

CLINICAL TRIALS

When sufficient preclinical data establishing the safety and pharmacology or efficacy are available, along with a good deal of other information about the new medical product under development, a petition may be filed with the FDA to obtain permission to evaluate the as yet unapproved (or uncleared) drug, biologic, or device in studies involving humans. Tests of this nature are known as clinical trials. For drugs and biologics, the application for permission to conduct clinical trials is

Table 9.1   Initial evaluation tests for consideration: biological evaluation of medical devices.

Device Categories			Biological Effect							
			Cytotoxicity	Sensitization	Irritation or Intracutaneous Reactivity	System Toxicity (Acute)	Subchronic toxicity (subacute toxicity)	Genotoxicity	Implantation	Haemocompatibility
Body contact		Contact duration (see 4.2) A—limited (24h) B—prolonged (24h to 30 days) C—permanent (>30 days)								
Surface devices	Skin	A	x	x	x	.	.	.	.	.
		B	x	x	x	.	.	.	.	.
		C	x	x	x	.	.	.	.	.
	Mucosal membrane	A	x	x	x	.	.	.	.	.
		B	x	x	x	o	o	.	o	.
		C	x	x	x	o	x	x	o	.
	Breached or compromised surfaces	A	x	x	x	o	.	.	.	.
		B	x	x	x	o	o	.	o	.
		C	x	x	x	o	x	x	o	.
External communicating devices	Blood path, indirect	A	x	x	x	x	.	.	.	x
		B	x	x	x	x	o	.	.	x
		C	x	x	o	x	x	x	o	x
	Tissue/bone/ dentin communicating+	A	x	x	x	o	.	.	.	.
		B	x	x	o	o	o	x	x	.
		C	x	x	o	o	o	x	x	.
	Circulating blood	A	x	x	x	x	.	o^	.	x
		B	x	x	x	x	o	x	o	x
		C	x	x	x	x	x	x	o	x
Implant devices	Tissue/bone	A	x	x	x	o	.	.	.	.
		B	x	x	o	o	o	x	x	.
		C	x	x	o	o	o	x	x	.
	Blood	A	x	x	x	x	.	.	x	x
		B	x	x	x	x	o	x	x	x
		C	x	x	x	x	x	x	x	x

X = ISO Evaluation Tests for Consideration
O = Additional Tests which may be applicable
Note + Tissue includes tissue fluids and subcutaneous spaces
Note ^ For all devices used in extracorporial circuits

Table 9.2　Supplementary evaluation tests for consideration: biological evaluation of medical devices.

Device Categories			Biological Effect			
Body Contact		Contact duration (see 4.2) A—limited (–24h) B—prolonged (24h to 30 days) C—permanent (>30 days)	Chronic Toxicity	Carcinogenicity	Reproductive Development	Biodegradable
Surface devices	Skin	A	.	.	.	.
		B	.	.	.	.
		C	.	.	.	.
	Mucosal membrane	A	.	.	.	.
		B	.	.	.	.
		C	o	.	.	.
	Breached or compromised surfaces	A	.	.	.	.
		B	.	.	.	.
		C	o	.	.	.
External communicating devices	Blood path, indirect	A	.	.	.	.
		B	.	.	.	.
		C	x	x	.	.
	Tissue/bone/ dentin communicating	A	.	.	.	.
		B	.	.	.	.
		C	o	x	.	.
	Circulating blood	A	.	.	.	.
		B	.	.	.	.
		C	x	x	.	.
Implant devices	Tissue/bone	A	.	.	.	.
		B	.	.	.	.
		C	x	x	.	.
	Blood	A	.	.	.	.
		B	.	.	.	.
		C	x	x	.	.

X = ISO Evaluation Tests for Consideration
O = Additional Tests which may be applicable

known as an IND application, while for medical devices, a request for an IDE is made. The format and content of INDs and IDEs have been discussed in chapter 2.

Although clinical trials have been conducted for decades within the context of quality systems known as good clinical practices (GCPs), international efforts to harmonize good clinical trial design are relatively recent. In August 1995, the FDA published draft guidelines on GCP under the auspices of the ICH.[43] The document defines GCP as an international ethical and scientific quality standard for designing, conducting, recording, and reporting trials that involve the participation of human subjects. This standard has its origin in the Declaration of Helsinki, a document dating back to 1964 and revised since, which embodies ethical and scientific principles for studies involving human subjects. The ICH guidance for GCP is intended to provide a unified standard to facilitate mutual acceptance of clinical data in the United States, the European Union, and Japan. Thirteen basic principles are described in the document, which stresses that quality assurance must be built into all aspects of a clinical study (see Figure 9.1). Both CDER and CBER were among the ICH sponsors of the guideline, which is directed to pharmaceutical studies. Nonetheless, the guideline is highly relevant to medical device clinical trials as well and, with time, the substance of the document is likely to hold considerable influence with CDRH and with the medical device review activities of international regulatory agencies.

FDA regulations require all research plans involving human testing of FDA-regulated medical products to be reviewed and approved by an institutional review board (IRB) before clinical testing can begin. These review boards exist in hospitals, academic centers, and research institutions at which clinical trials take place. An IRB also conducts at least an annual review throughout the duration of an approved clinical trial. The purpose of

1. Clinical trials should be conducted in accordance with the ethical principles that have their origin in the Declaration of Helsinki, and that are consistent with GCP and the applicable regulatory requirement(s).

2. Before a trial is initiated, foreseeable risks and inconveniences should be weighed against the anticipated benefit for the individual trial subject and society. A trial should be initiated and continued only if the anticipated benefits justify the risks.

continued

Figure 9.1 Principles of ICH GCP.

continued

3. The rights, safety, and well-being of the trial subjects are the most important considerations and should prevail over interests of science and society.

4. The available nonclinical and clinical information on an investigational product should be adequate to support the proposed clinical trial.

5. Clinical trials should be scientifically sound, and described in a clear, detailed protocol.

6. A trial should be conducted in compliance with the protocol and amendment(s) that have received prior institutional review board (IRB)/independent ethics committee (IEC) approval/favorable opinion.

7. The medical care given to, and medical decisions made for, subjects should always be the responsibility of a qualified physician or, when appropriate, of a qualified dentist.

8. Each individual involved in conducting a trial should be qualified by education, training, and experience to perform his or her respective task(s).

9. Freely given informed consent should be obtained from every subject prior to clinical trial participation.

10. All clinical trial information should be recorded, handled, and stored in a way that allows its accurate reporting, interpretation, and verification.

11. The confidentiality of records that could identify subjects should be protected, respecting the privacy and confidentiality rules in accordance with the applicable regulatory requirement(s).

12. Investigational products should be manufactured, handled, and stored in accordance with applicable good manufacturing practice (GMP). They should be used in accordance with the approved protocol and amendment(s).

13. Systems with procedures that assure the quality of every aspect of the trial should be implemented.

Figure 9.1   Principles of ICH GCP.

the IRB review is to ensure that risks to subjects are minimized, informed consent is obtained and documented for each subject, selection of subjects is fair and equitable, risks to subjects are reasonable in relation to expected benefit, and that privacy and confidentiality of subjects are protected. At least five people with varying backgrounds make up an IRB. They are usually knowledgeable in the relevant research areas, but at least one member must be in a nonscientific discipline, and at least one member must not be affiliated with the institution. An IRB may refuse to allow a clinical trial to be conducted at its institution if it perceives the study as not safe enough or as not providing any therapeutic benefit to the patient.

Clinical trials of drugs and biologic pharmaceuticals typically consist of three phases:

• *Phase I* (sometimes Arabic numerals are used, rather than Roman numerals), involving a relatively small number of healthy volunteers, is geared toward determining side effects and gathering initial safety information. If everything goes appropriately in Phase I, the test material may go on to the next phase.

• *Phase II* trials involve a larger number of subjects who have the condition the product is intended to treat. Phase II trials are often—indeed ideally—double-blind (neither the investigator nor the patient knows whether the investigational treatment or a control is used), randomized, controlled trials and are designed to determine optimal dosage levels and to detect short-term side effects. If a test product makes it through Phase II, it is moved into Phase III.

• *Phase III* trials involve large numbers of subjects—thousands—usually in double-blind, randomized, controlled studies that are often conducted at multiple test sites. In Phase III, detailed data are gathered about the effectiveness of the pharmaceutical in comparison to control treatments. Subjects are followed to evaluate long-term side effects and safety.

At the conclusion of the clinical trials (assuming all has gone well), an NDA is submitted to the FDA requesting approval to market a new drug. In the case of a biologic, the submission for marketing approval is a BLA. Figure 9.2 provides an overview of the new drug development and approval process. Out-of-pocket costs for new drug clinical trials have been reported as ranging from $50 million to $89 million, depending on the size of the drug company.[44]

The *common technical document (CTD)* is one aspect of ICH efforts with regard to the harmonization of requirements for the approval of pharmaceuticals. The FDA has exerted considerable effort in the development of the ICH drug application document known as the CTD.[45] The CTD is

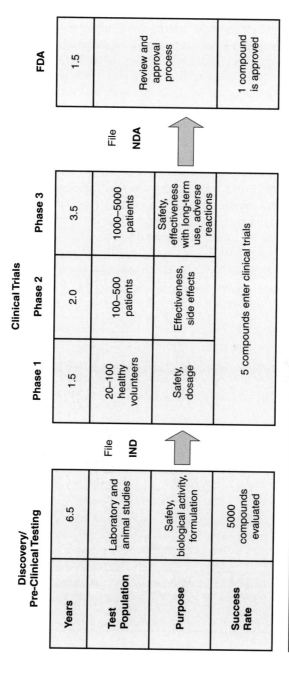

Figure 9.2 Overview of the new drug clinical development process.
Adapted from: New Drug Approvals in 2002, PhRMA

a prescribed organization of the information required to be submitted to a regulatory authority, and as such represents an application format, but not to an application type. The CTD certainly does not define the requirements, quality, or quantity of content of an application. Indeed, there are many regional requirements, as well as applicants' preferences, that will affect the contents of a CTD submitted in each ICH region. Thus, according to FDA, the BLA and the NDA will not disappear with the adoption of the CTD format. Unlike the European Union and Japan, the United States does not plan to make the use of the CTD mandatory. The agency does, however, hope that use of the CTD format will help to standardize the presentation of information in drug and biologics applications, and thus make review a bit easier. The harmonized document comprises five modules, as shown in Figure 9.3.

Although conducting clinical trials has a long-established history when it comes to drugs, the situation is quite different when it comes to medical devices. In the mid-1990s, only approximately 10 percent of all medical device submissions to CDRH included clinical data as part of the scientific evidence in support of product claims. The FDA has taken steps toward

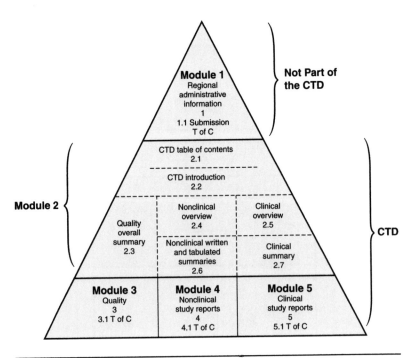

Figure 9.3 Diagrammatic representation of the ICH common technical document.

imposing more stringent requirements for clinical trials that are used in support of Class III devices requiring PMAs. Clinical studies are also increasingly required in support of certain Class II medical device 510(k) submissions.

There are significant differences in the logistics of conducting clinical trials on medical devices. Blinding is often not possible in device studies. For example, it may be impossible to arrange for a surgeon not to be able to ascertain whether she or he is using an investigational device, since a sugar-pill placebo or sham version of a three-dimensional functional mechanical item—especially if it is used to perform a therapeutic action or if it is an implantable device—simply may not be possible to create and use safely or ethically. Choosing appropriate controls for controlled medical device studies is also more problematic than selecting controls for drug or biologics clinical studies. In drug studies, controls usually consist of a placebo, which has no biological activity, or another drug that has already been approved for the condition being treated. The subject can, for example, take a pill or get a shot, and neither the subject nor the investigator will know whether what has been administered is the test agent or control. But controls for medical device trials can be older versions of the same device, different devices that have been approved or cleared, devices that look the same as the test device but do not deliver therapy (shams), nondevice therapies, or no therapy at all—all of which are commonly discernable to the investigator. Here are some other unique aspects of medical device clinical trials:

- Compared to drug studies, medical device trials tend to involve relatively few subjects, although each subject might require a longer follow-up.

- Use of a device is often just part of a complex therapeutic procedure.

- The success of the procedure frequently depends on factors other than the device, such as the skill of a surgeon or the extent of a surgical intervention.

- Clinical trials of some in vitro diagnostic devices may not require an IDE at all, provided that the testing is noninvasive, does not require an invasive sampling procedure that presents significant risk, does not introduce energy into a subject, and is not used as a diagnostic procedure without confirmation of the diagnosis by another medically established product or procedure.

- There are different requirements for what the FDA considers significant-risk devices and nonsignificant-risk devices.

Traditional Phase I studies on medical devices are often not possible. Devices that are used invasively, for example, or that deliver radiation, would be inappropriate for use in safety evaluations on healthy volunteers. There is a greater tendency to view device trials as being small-scale *feasibility* or *pilot* studies (sometimes also referred to as Phase II) or as being the larger scope *pivotal studies* (often referred to as Phase III).

In order to resolve issues such as device design, device operation, and patient population, the FDA encourages medical device companies to conduct small-scale pilot or feasibility studies prior to initiating a pivotal clinical trial—a pivotal trial being one that will yield the clinical data used to support a submission for approval or clearance. A pilot study usually involves fewer than 20 patients, while a pivotal device trial may involve several hundred patients and often is conducted at multiple sites.

After a successful clinical trial, a PMA application for marketing approval or a 510(k) application for marketing clearance is filed with the FDA, depending upon the device class and requirements.

When a medical product has been approved or cleared for marketing by the FDA, it is not uncommon to conduct focused, limited clinical studies referred to as *Phase IV* studies. These studies are generally conducted to support marketing efforts by generating additional performance or economic data, often for publication, or by cultivating and involving key customers.

Many medical products companies engage the services of a contract research organization (CRO) to assist in the planning, execution, and follow-up of clinical trials. CROs provide a wide variety of services, such as protocol development, data management and analysis, and preparation of FDA submission documents. It is virtually impossible for a small company to independently conduct a clinical trial, and even large companies often use CROs for selected tasks.

DIVERSITY IN CLINICAL TRIALS

Variations in response to medical products and procedures have been observed among distinct groups within the population of the United States. Age, gender, size, and ethnic origin can independently or collectively influence the effects of medical and surgical treatments. With some procedures, these factors do not seem to matter or need to be taken into account at all. The same volume dose of influenza vaccine is used whether the patent weighs 95 pounds or 295 pounds, whether male or female. But weight and gender have considerable implications on the use of anesthesia in surgery.

The reasons for the diverse responses to medical treatments are manifold, and appear to include both known and probable intrinsic and extrinsic factors, or a combination of the two. Intrinsic factors primarily reflect the effect of genetic or physiologic differences, while extrinsic factors are tied to environment. Pharmacogenetic research has uncovered significant differences associated with race or ethnicity in the metabolism, clinical effectiveness, and side-effect profiles of many drugs.

Unfortunately, the medical products industry has not yet been able to get its arms around this issue. Unless a product is specifically designed for use within a population subgroup, the subjects of clinical trials for drugs, biologics, and medical devices have tended to be rather homogeneous. Historically, women and children have been neglected in clinical trials, and ethnicity of patients has been rarely recorded, much less evaluated for association with treatment response. Consequently, the specific treatment requirements and responses of the very young, the very old, women, and minority Americans—especially those of African, Asian, and Hispanic heritage— have been ignored. Partly for this reason, substantial disparities exist in the quality and quantity of medical care received by these population subsets. FDA has recently begun to address ethnic diversity in clinical trials by providing industry with opinions and guidances.[46]

By encouraging diversity as a factor to be included at all stages of development of a medical product, the FDA hopes that industry and the FDA will be better positioned to understand how medical products will affect different populations when they reach the market. Information that is gathered during development and clinical evaluations can then be used to refine product labeling, patient selection, and dose selection. The desired outcome is the marketing of safer and more effective medical products.

One final point for consideration in product development planning: choose clinical endpoints carefully, with focus on appropriate, convincing measures of the clinical effect that you wish to evaluate. The difference in efficacy of your test product, compared to the control treatment, may be *statistically* significant, but not *clinically* significant. The endpoint must accurately represent a clinical characteristic that is worthy of medical intervention.

10

How Much Is the Product Really Worth?

Outcomes Research, Pharmacoeconomics, and Managed Care

Not everything that can be counted counts, and not everything that counts can be counted.

—Albert Einstein

Everything is worth what its purchaser will pay for it.

—Publius Syrus

There is pronounced interest in how the vast healthcare expenditures in the United States are being directed, and whether there is really value in terms of effects on health and on society as a result of these expenditures. In an environment of both escalating healthcare expenditures and limited funding resources, cost-containment has become a major concern for patients, healthcare providers, and insurance payers. Therefore, it is becoming more and more important for clinical trials of all types of medical products to be designed to address outcomes other than simply functional clinical efficacy and safety. Today there is a higher demand for products that will also provide positive outcomes in terms of clinical utility, cost-effectiveness, and quality of life. The need is obvious if one considers that it has been estimated that only 10 percent to 20 percent of all medical procedures performed in the United States have ever been proved effective in randomized controlled clinical trials.[47]

Outcomes research comprises studies that are conducted in order to measure the end result of medical treatment and the effect of that treatment on the health and well-being of patients.

Compared to clinical research, which evaluates the safety and efficacy of medical technology, outcomes research examines whether the technology increases survival, reduces morbidity, improves any number of aspects of quality of life, and provides benefits that justify the costs of its use. Ideally risk–benefit ratios should take priority over cost concerns. Costs, in turn, should include cost-effectiveness analyses that assess not only the immediate outcome and associated costs, but also the long-term effects and results of treatment and the impact on future costs and societal benefits.

Two powerful forces are driving the trend to conduct outcomes research: (1) reforms to healthcare provider systems, especially that phenomenon known as *managed care,* and (2) the astounding rate of technological, biotechnological, and procedural advances, which increase the number of available options in the practice of healthcare.

Managed care refers to healthcare provided by a prepaid health plan or covered by an insurance program, in which medical services for covered patients are reviewed and coordinated with the intent of managing access to care, quality of care, and cost of care.

The overriding concern for cost containment is approached through a variety of ways, such as closed formularies (restricting the therapeutic agents that will be covered or reimbursed); requiring the use of generic drugs whenever they are available; using primary-care physicians as "gatekeepers" to make decisions about treatment or referral to specialists; and relying on outcomes research to provide standards for acceptance and coverage of medical treatments, including the use of drugs, biologics, and medical devices. Many people might argue that managed care is actually a contraction of, "you're lucky if you *managed* to get any *care* at all."

As yet, there are no national, much less international, standards for outcomes evaluations. Although there is sloppiness in the consistency of terminology and in consensus of opinion, outcomes research has primarily concentrated on various types of economic analyses and on quality of life measurements. Economic analyses of medical products attempt to answer questions about the use of the products, such as:

- What are the direct and indirect costs of the intervention?

- What are the costs compared to those associated with the use of other products?

- What are the cost savings related to reduced need for medical follow-up or additional treatment?

- What are the cost advantages of avoiding hospitalization?
- What is the economic impact of earlier return of the patient to the workforce?
- What is the economic impact of lives saved?
- What are the costs associated with early diagnosis?
- What is the economic impact of disease prevention?

CLINICAL OUTCOMES

Clinical outcomes are the results of a medical intervention in planned, controlled studies. The basic assumption is that the clinical differences observed between a treatment group and a control group are due to the treatment. The evaluation of clinical safety and efficacy through the clinical trials process is discussed in chapter 9. In real life, as opposed to controlled clinical trials, many uncontrollable and even unidentifiable factors affect the clinical benefits of a medical product. The physical environment and location, experience of practitioners, health status of the patient, and concomitant medical treatment of the patient are a few of the variables that can hinder or help the clinical outcomes derived from a medical product. Information on real-life product effectiveness is generated through post-marketing surveillance and reports.

PHARMACOECONOMICS AND ECONOMIC OUTCOMES

A basic definition of pharmacoeconomics is: the application of economic principles to the evaluation of pharmaceutical therapy interventions. Through a comparison of costs and consequences of the use of various pharmaceutical products and services, the objective of pharmacoeconomic analysis is to improve public health through improved, rational decision making. The major analytical methods used in pharmacoeconomic analyses are cost-effectiveness analysis (CEA), cost-minimization analysis (CMA), cost/utility analysis (CUA) and cost/benefit analysis (CBA).[48] Recently, there has been growing interest in applying the principles of pharmacoeconomics to evaluate the economics of use of all medical products, as well as medical and surgical procedures. Examples of economic analysis techniques are shown in Table 10.1.

Table 10.1 Pharmacoeconomic methods.

Method	Objective
Cost-effectiveness analysis (CEA)	Compare costs and consequences of two alternative treatments, with costs measured in monetary terms and effectiveness measured in outcome units. A cost-effective treatment may not be less expensive if it provides additional benefit that is worth the extra cost.
Cost-minimization analysis (CMA)	Determine the least expensive alternative among products with equivalent safety and efficacy. This is the simplest method of analysis.
Cost/utility analysis (CUA)	Compare costs and consequences of a treatment with costs measured in monetary units, and consequences measured in terms of patient preferences of one outcome over another (often expressed in terms of QOL)
Cost/benefit analysis (CBA)	Measure costs and benefits, all of which are expressed in monetary units. CBA requires the conversion of disparate outcomes into standard monetary units and can be used to determine which choice has the greater potential to benefit society, based on resource allotment.

Table 10.2 Examples of quality of life domains.

Domain	Attributes
Physical health	Symptoms, pain
Mental health	Well-being, life satisfaction, anxiety, depression, cognitive functioning
Social functioning	Personal and community interactions
Role functioning	Work, task, and household management
General health perceptions	Satisfaction with healthcare, energy

QUALITY OF LIFE OUTCOMES

Quality of life (QOL) assessments comprise evaluations of patient-oriented factors. The relevant domains are related to the status of the patient's physical and mental health, functional status, and general health perceptions (see Table 10.2). Although life-quality factors are extremely important, they are difficult to measure quantitatively. QOL depends upon an individual's perceptions, beliefs, feelings and expectations. The person's own appraisal of his or her health and well-being is a key factor in QOL studies. Questionnaires and interviews are common tools to evaluate QOL outcomes, and results are thus subject to collection and interpretation being influenced by culture, gender, age, and honesty. Furthermore, the individual appraisals must be consistent and reproducible enough to be extrapolated to an entire patient population.

OUTCOMES AND PRODUCT DEVELOPMENT PLANNING

When planning for or developing a new product, it is important for the entire organization to understand the purpose of the product, and to consider the marketing wish list for that product. In early stages of development, desired outcomes are highly relevant to product design. Remember, form follows function (well, usually). Planning for appropriate preclinical evaluations and developing the treatment models for preclinical efficacy studies should be geared toward all clinical outcomes of interest. Finally, the clinical trials themselves must be designed to encompass endpoints that will demonstrate, if successful, the desired outcomes.

In the selection of outcomes, the product development planning team must ask and answer the questions:

- What would we like to know?

- What would we like to show?

- Is it likely to be worth the development to know or show?

- Is there a great likelihood that the product will provide either: (1) a benefit that will justify higher cost, or (2) benefits comparable to existing therapies at a lower cost?

Regardless of the category, any outcomes measure should ideally be:

- Directly associated with a benefit to the patient

- Relevant to the medical treatment

- Unambiguous and definable

- Mutually exclusive to alternative outcomes

- Quantifiable

- Reproducible in repeated treatments

- Statistically significant

Outcomes evaluations of one sort or another have been misused by some medical products manufacturers in order to create a marketing edge. It has been far too routine to see or hear advertisements for products that claim to be better, safer, and more cost-effective than competitive products. QOL outcomes are implied by words and pictures of people feeling more energetic, smarter, and happier as a result of using a product. This is an ethical and legal issue if the claims are unsubstantiated and misleading. The FDA currently expects outcomes claims to be based on well-controlled clinical trials. Well-established guidelines will help to eliminate the skepticism that can arise when a company has a vested interest in the pharmacoeconomic analysis of its own product. Nevertheless, the enormous investments in medical product development, coupled with risks in marketability, constitute a powerful incentive for manufacturers to obtain economic data to support new products.

Meanwhile, healthcare reform and evolving controversies over resource allocations, drug pricing, and reimbursement will demand more rigorous data to justify expenditures based on clinical and humanistic outcomes as well as cost. While the FDA, as yet, has no formal defined policy or requirement for outcomes research and purports to have no concern about product costs when reviewing submissions, the agency has expressed strong interest in seeing data demonstrating clinical utility, comparative efficacy, and QOL outcomes. We can expect to see interest in outcomes research continue to increase, and should be ever aware that outcomes issues need to be included in product development planning.

Part III

Product Development Planning

11

Models and Metaphors

Product Development and the Product Development Organization

Plans are nothing, but planning is everything.

—Attributed to Napoleon Bonaparte

Every idea has something of the pain and peril of child-birth about it.

—Samuel Butler

The concept of product development is often schematically presented as a horizontal or vertical funnel (see Figure 11.1). This structure illustrates the principle that a successful development strategy starts out with a multitude of new product ideas. These ideas are represented by numerous inclusions at the wide end of the funnel. Each idea can be thought of as a potential project, and thus as a possible future product. Since there are always more potential projects than there are financial or human resources to allot to them, the ideas are subjected to some type of scrutiny, selectively eliminating those that are less desirable or feasible while retaining those most worthy of pursuit. Eventually, the idea pool is narrowed enough that a significant investment can be made to bring a few of the most promising projects through development and on to product launch. Launched new products are depicted as blebs exiting the narrow end of the funnel.[49,50]

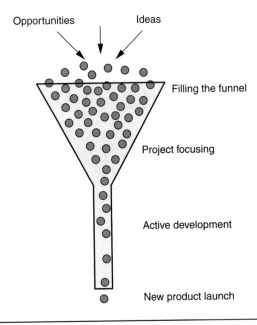

Figure 11.1   Stylized new product development funnel.

Depending on the nature of a given business, the project-focusing process may require hundreds of possibilities entering the open end of the funnel in order to yield just one commercializable product from the narrow end of the funnel. This is especially true in the pharmaceutical industry, when molecular modeling and trial-and-error screening can involve the consideration of a vast number of drug candidates. In any given segment of the medical device industry, the numbers are likely to be quite different, with perhaps 10 to 100 ideas potentially available to enter the funnel.

In the development of FDA-regulated medical products, the number of new products emerging from the funnel depends on a variety of internal and external factors. Technical feasibility is one. An idea may be incredibly interesting, but not realistically achievable within the century—which may be longer than the company cares to wait. Similarly, a market opportunity for an idea may or may not exist now or be likely to exist when the idea could become an actual new product. There are numerous issues and hurdles that must be identified and assessed.

Models of this sort often make things look too easy. Product development appears too automatic a process. The models seem to suggest that the hardest part of product development is choosing from among the dozens, scores, or hundreds of opportunities waiting in the wings. The models, in other words, seem to suggest a guaranteed outcome of commercialized products as long as one does a good job of drawing a funnel.

SWIMMING AGAINST THE STREAM

The development of new FDA-regulated medical products is an uphill struggle with no guarantees. A more appropriate metaphor for a model would be that of salmon swimming upstream, against incredible odds, to spawn and assure the continuance of the species. Salmon swim upstream, from ocean to fresh water, for distances of up to 2000 miles on a journey that may take months. In their fight against rushing currents, 10-foot waterfalls, and treacherous rapids, there are significant casualties. Weak fish become exhausted and are washed away with the flow of the rushing water. Others are dashed against rocks or fail to clear obstacles in the stream, becoming stranded and doomed to die. Bears lurk on the banks, knocking the fish out of the water and greedily devouring them. Then there are the sport and commercial fishermen waiting for their take. It's not an easy trip.

Let's consider how this natural adventure relates to medical product development, with the trip upstream signifying the development pathway and spawning signifying the launch of new products. This allows the business (the species) to go on. The masses of oceanic salmon on their way to spawn represent the large idea and opportunity pool, and the current coursing against them represents changing, evolving elements that impede progress. Large rocks and rapids are factors in the internal and external environment that we recognize and over which we may even have some degree of control. Finally, the grizzly bears and fishermen stand for conditions in the internal and external environment over which we (that is, the product developers) have no control. Examples of various types of impediments are given in Figures 11.2 to 11.5.

In this model, the role of a defined product development process with documented design controls is to minimize the negative impact of certain obstacles by serving in part (to be consistent with the model) as a fish ladder. Fish ladders are artificial sloping waterfalls that are built to help the salmon travel over dams and other virtually nonnegotiable areas. The ladder of process will increase the likelihood of survival of the fittest projects and maximize the opportunity of those projects to be transformed into successful, profitable new products. Additionally, a sound product development process will provide navigational maps identifying the location and magnitude of

Rocks—navigate by knowledge and planning

- Costs
- Design creep
- Reluctance to kill hopeless projects
- Lack of processes
- Enslavement by processes
- Design flaws
- Insufficient intellectual property protection
- Too many meetings
- Too few meetings
- Poorly trained teams
- Not planning for future technologies
- Insufficient knowledge of regulatory issues
- No formal product development planning
- Team conflict
- Too many projects
- Wrong skill sets
- Wrong mix of projects
- Unclear product concept
- Not prioritizing projects
- Lack of formal reviews
- Lack of focus on quality

Figure 11.2   Internal impediments to medical product development that can be controlled or influenced by a product development organization (salmon swimming upstream analogy).

hazards and will help provide the knowledge and facility necessary to avoid or overcome obstacles.

While more evocative of the challenges, obstacles, and hazards confronting medical product development, this model is somewhat extravagant and certainly unconventional. For the sake of simplicity, though,

Strong opposing currents—swim against the stream with strength, organization, and courage

- Corporate bureaucracy
- Not enough money
- Not enough people
- Not enough time
- No senior management representation
- Lack of senior management commitment
- Physical separation of team members
- Inadequate technology base or core competencies
- Bad attitude about regulatory and quality requirements
- Management turnover
- Unrealistic expectations
- Unclear business objectives
- Reorganization
- Restructuring
- Reengineering

Figure 11.3   Internal impediments to medical product development that are not usually controlled or significantly influenced by a product development organization (salmon swimming upstream analogy).

reference to funnel models will be the norm in later discussions of the product development process.

THE CROSS-FUNCTIONAL ORGANIZATION

What, then, does it take for a healthcare company to guide and propel new product opportunities through the treacherous and labyrinthine course that lies ahead? It takes a talented, committed multidisciplinary product development organization, with each member qualified for his

Rapids and waterfalls—avoid or know ahead of time how
to negotiate

- Competitors (some)
- Reluctant customers
- Decreasing product lifecycles
- Premature obsolescence by new technologies
- Unclear fit with customer/market needs
- Negative image from past product problems
- Poor rapport with FDA
- Unreceptive marketplace
- Vendor/supply problems

Figure 11.4 External impediments to medical product development
that can be controlled or influenced by a product development organization
(salmon swimming upstream analogy).

Grizzlies and other predators—be aware and be prepared

- Vague/changing FDA requirements
- Differing global requirements
- Outcomes requirements
- Managed care
- Other unpredictable new health/medical issues
- Competitors (some)
- International cultural biases
- Emerging or new diseases
- Ageing/expiring patents
- Healthcare reform

Figure 11.5 External impediments to medical product development that are
not usually controlled or influenced by a product development organization
(salmon swimming upstream analogy).

or her responsibilities through education, training, and experience (see Figure 11.6). The first paradigm shift that has to take place is not to equate or confuse "product development" with the "development" in R&D. To be sure, R&D people are important elements in a product development organization—as are development scientists (which, depending on the nature of the products, can include biologists, chemists, physicists, computer scientists, engineers, or others) and participants with experience and expertise in marketing, manufacturing, quality assurance, regulatory affairs, clinical evaluations, new business development, and other functions. Product development is a cross-functional activity, and as such requires the involvement of a cross-functional group sharing the same goals: identification, development, and launch of new products. This does not at all mean that there must or even should be a separate product development department within a company (although separate product development departments can work very well). What it does mean is that without the participation of individuals with a variety of specific functional abilities—that is, without involvement of a cross-functional group—healthcare product development efforts will be next to worthless. This is the most fundamental requirement.

By the way, one functional area that is often overlooked or underestimated is responsibility for and capability of assessing technology. It is an easy and mistaken assumption that conventional new business development departments take care of this. Many business development associates are splendid at identifying opportunities, but lack the knowledge of the scientific, regulatory, and market nuance issues that profoundly affect the opportunity. To have someone with these skills working with business development

- Commitment to quality
- Cross-functional participation
- Technology assessment capability
- Concurrent (parallel) development approach
- Group knowledge of regulatory issues
- Upper-level management representation
- Immediate access to information resources
- Clear understanding of where the buck stops

Figure 11.6 What a product development organization needs.

associates or, indeed, working in the capacity of business development, makes for a much more powerful and effective tool when it comes to searching for new opportunities.

Some companies do not have resource representation in all of the functional areas that may be critical to the products they are trying to develop. If the required skill sets are not on hand, or if certain skills are needed only infrequently, consultants can provide a satisfactory solution. Consultants may be independent and from the outside, they may be internal to a company and available *ad hoc* to various product development initiatives, or they may be available through lending out of expert associates of affiliate companies. The important thing is to have people with the necessary skills readily available and involved in the new product development efforts.

Much has been written and discussed in recent years about the advantages of concurrent engineering in product development. Simply put, concurrent engineering or parallel development refers to the simultaneous as well as sequential integrated execution of tasks by various functional participants in the product development process. This approach differs from the "handing-off" system in which one function—for example, R&D—does what it considers its part and then hands off the project to another group, such as manufacturing. Manufacturing may then hand off to regulatory affairs, which hands off to marketing, which hands the responsibility over to sales. Concurrent engineering works best. Some companies, however, prefer to employ the sequential hand-off approach, often because of deeply entrenched habits and history. Medical product development can succeed in this environment if there is sufficient cross-functional project planning and if documentation and progress are frequently reviewed by a responsible cross-functional group.

Two other aspects that are very important to successful product development are convenient access to a well-stocked electronic library with subscriptions to as many relevant periodicals as possible, and the requirement for all participants in the product development organization to understand regulatory issues and quality standards. It is perplexing that so many otherwise respectable healthcare manufacturers cut costs by eliminating subscriptions and access to document search and retrieval resources. If something sparks in your mind and you need information now to satisfy the itch, you need the information *now*. In a day or two, the itch will be gone or you'll have forgotten why you were so interested in the first place. Momentum will be lost and opportunities will vanish.

A word about regulatory and quality affairs: they are inextricable and they are everybody's business. The medical products industry is too sensitive to regulatory issues to assume that product development can proceed smoothly as long as a regulatory affairs specialist is nominally on hand. In fact, the performance of that specialist will suffer unless everyone involved with product development is cognizant of the regulatory environment and understands, for example, the difference between guidelines and regulations. Organizations also may have misconceptions about quality functions. Quality is not just an attribute of a finished, manufactured product indicating that it meets some set of product specifications. It cannot be simply considered a postdevelopment issue, and personnel involved in quality functions must be included in premanufacturing product development activities. Quality has to be built into a product by being incorporated into the product development process. Remember, domestic and international standards now require that quality systems include the design phase of product development.

Finally, in the seemingly never-ending quest to turn around a lagging or failing business, companies are periodically and regularly reinventing, reorganizing, restructuring, and reengineering. Such companies are very likely struggling because they are not developing any new products or they are developing the wrong products. Both problems are indicative of inadequate, dysfunctional, or absent product development processes, product development organizations, and product development support. Yet, surprisingly, the revised organizational structure may end up having no upper management representation for product development. In the realm of FDA-regulated medical products, product development needs a champion at a level that is heard and that carries influence. Development is less effective if upper management responsibility is left to another specific functional representative who has all of the company responsibilities for that particular area to worry about, or to a nontechnical business generalist who has to put out daily fires and worry about the quotidian bottom line. To remain or to become known for excellence in product development, a medical products company should be eager to show its commitment and support through high-level management responsibility and representation for product development. It is as important for that responsible individual to be able to participate firsthand, on a daily basis, with other functional and business executives in discussions of business issues and strategic direction as it is to be an advocate for the product development organization and product development process. It makes a great deal of sense to have intimate management leadership provided by someone who can concentrate on creating tomorrow's business and who is not preoccupied with all of the distractions of managing and running today's business.

With a talented and trained product development organization in place, a medical products company will be in a position to implement product development planning. The first important steps will have been taken for providing a steady stream of profitable new products.

12

Components of Product Development Planning

The Product Development Process

Begin at the beginning.., and go on till you come to the end: then stop.

—Lewis Carroll

Never mistake motion for action.

—Ernest Hemingway

The product development process is one of the four integral components of product development planning (see Figure 12.1). It is also the component of product development planning that is most firmly grounded in the present, because its implementation requires the existence of one or more ideas or opportunities upon which a product development organization can act.

Product development is generally thought of as a series of steps or phases, beginning with a product idea or opportunity and ending with the launch of a new product. Often, an analogy is drawn to human development in utero, with conception, gestation, and labor and delivery representing the phases of product development. While valid in some respects, the analogy neglects some very important points.

Despite the division into stages and trimesters and such, in utero development occurs through a continuum of processes and doesn't happen in a saltatory fashion. Although conception may be the official initiating event,

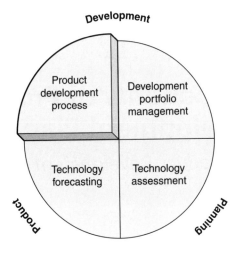

Figure 12.1   The product development process is an integral component of product development planning.

it is preceded by an actionable idea, and it must be enabled by physiologically capable bodies. If, following conception, a complex myriad of interacting factors work together in concert, gestation proceeds and a healthy baby is born. But to remain viable, the baby requires nurturing, monitoring, and support.

The product development process is also a continuum of activities, starting with the light bulb that is switched on in someone's prepared mind (an occurrence enabled by intelligent and supportive management) and ending with the early support activities that follow the introduction of the new product into the marketplace. In between, a complex myriad of interacting factors must work together in concert. It is the responsibility of the product development organization to make sure that it happens.

For the sake of convenience, it is helpful to identify some of the infinite number of steps that make up the continuum of product development:

- Idea generation

- Concept evaluation

- Feasibility testing

- Product definition

- Design development

- Risk analysis

- Design optimization

- Prototyping

- Confirmative testing

- Pilot production

- Scale-up

- Production

- Launch

- Follow-through

The objective of establishing a product development process divided into discreet phases is to: (1) provide discipline and consistency for internal review and portfolio analysis; (2) establish a product development system, focused on quality, with formal design review milestones to comply with design controls requirements/recommendations of FDA GMPs; and (3) to facilitate eventual marketing of developed products outside of the United States by meeting international standards for design control. There is no reason to duplicate efforts, so a well-constructed product development process will accomplish all of the objectives simultaneously. As a bonus, implementation and action on such a process will greatly improve the likelihood of developing a product that is right for the customers, right for the company, cost-effective, manufactured with quality, and free of design defects. And once the process is understood, accepted, and supported by those involved in product development and by management, shortened development time will be a reality.

It wouldn't be realistic for most product development organizations to employ a process with as many phases as indicated previously. Some of these elements tend to fall together into natural groupings. The number of groupings and the elements included in each can be customized according to the nature of the products being developed by the organization. Think about what makes sense in terms of review frequency for the protection of the patients, the security of the company, and the satisfaction of the FDA. If a very simple product is being developed, if it is not unique and is fabricated from common and conventional materials, and if the company has the appropriate core competencies to develop and make the product, two or three reviews before launch might be adequate and acceptable. If the product idea involves complex, largely untested technologies and carries with it a high degree of financial, technological, regulatory, market, or safety risk, 10 formal reviews might be a good idea.

For some Class II and most Class III medical devices, and for drugs and biologics of comparable complexity, it would be wise to use at least six product development phases along with five reviews, three of which are formal design reviews (see Table 12.1). Remember that for medical devices, the schedule for design review and the output of these reviews will become part of the company's permanent design control process and file to demonstrate adherence to QSRs (that is, device GMPs). For the purpose of illustration and future discussion, then, we will consider a generic six-phase medical product development process:

- Phase 1—Discovery

- Phase 2—Feasibility

- Phase 3—Optimization

- Phase 4—Demonstration

- Phase 5—Production

- Phase 6—Launch and follow-through

At the end of each phase, a review system functions as a screen or filter, allowing the projects with the greatest potential to pass through to the next phase, while excluding those with less potential. Figure 12.2 illustrates the application of this process to the product development funnel model.

Table 12.1 Six-step healthcare product development process.

Product Development Phase	Review at Phase Completion
1. *Discovery:* generation of ideas and search for opportunities	Management approval
2. *Feasibility:* concept testing and evaluation of likelihood of success	Design review committee/ management
3. *Optimization:* development and refinement of product design	Design review committee: formal design review
4. *Demonstration:* confirmation of safety and effectiveness	Design review committee: formal design review
5. *Production:* scale-up to commercial-level manufacturing	Design review committee: formal design review
6. *Launch and follow-through:* introduction into market and support of the new product	

Figure 12.2 The product development process.

PHASE 1—DISCOVERY

The unrestrained generation and accumulation of ideas takes place during the discovery phase. It is a time for exploration, ideation, suggestion, brainstorming, and investigation. Each idea is a potential new product concept. The ideal situation for a product development organization to be in is to have a surplus of ideas in relation to the number of projects it can actually pursue. It is through discovery that possibilities enter the wide, open end of the hypothetical product development funnel.

Conventional product development literature frequently recommends determining what customers' needs are, then seeking ideas that might provide solutions. Or conventional approaches may insist that all exploratory searches start with an analysis of the industry under consideration for a product entry. It is frequently suggested, too, that all ideas sought should be compatible with core capabilities, such as specific scientific or manufacturing expertise. In the medical products industry, strict adherence to these tenets may be unwise. It constrains one to view the future through the veil of a preconceived present.

In the first place, customers don't always know what their needs are. This is true for both patients and medical professionals. As consumers, we should all be able to think of some product or technology that has entered and changed our lives for the better. Before that product became available, we had never given a thought to the technology or to the need it would serve, but now we wonder how we ever got along without it. Today, we may recognize microwave ovens, personal computers, electronic networking, and word processing software as falling into this category. In the past, electric lights and penicillin would have qualified. If a product development organization is going to beat its competitors to the future, it has to take off the blinders and be receptive to ideas and opportunities that may, at first blush, seem outlandish, inappropriate, or inconsequential. Those involved in product development must be prepared to lead customers into the future by offering products for which those customers might not, on their own, have recognized or articulated a need.

By collecting ideas only within the context of an industry analysis, a medical product company can be fairly sure that it will be left behind, buried beneath the dust kicked up by open-minded competitors with foresight as they race to the market with successful new products. Consider the dizzying advances in diagnostic abilities, recombinant genetic technology, tissue engineering, microsurgery and minimally invasive surgery, robotics, and the stunning challenges presented by reemerging or newly emerging or unidentified diseases, not to mention politically and economically sensitive issues such as healthcare reform and managed care. Anyone presuming to be able to get to the future with medical devices, drugs, or biologics products by using ideation based on the industry and market as we now know it, or as we might anticipate it to be in the short-term future, belongs in a different business.

Finally, the admission of an idea into the discovery phase should not be predicated solely on the basis of the core competencies of a company—even though core competencies are an important element in product development planning. Successful companies do not remain static. New competencies can be built, acquired, or contracted if an idea or project is important enough.

Remember, just because an idea is in the pool in the discovery phase doesn't absolutely mean it's going to become a project. There will be ample opportunity to apply restrictions, hurdles, and other screening procedures. A seemingly inappropriate idea may spark another idea or may set off a chain reaction of ideas, and a terrific new product opportunity could be the result.

Ideas can include the likes of novel concepts, suggestions for differentiated line extensions, suggestions to go after or take advantage of licensing opportunities, and proposals for acquisitions. Ideas may come from just about anywhere—from R&D, marketing, or any other company group;

customers and competitors; technical and patent literature; technology transfer groups; academia; newspaper and magazine articles; conventions, sym-
posia and professional meetings; one's children; or dreams. The ideas are
assessed according to predetermined and agreed-upon criteria for advancement to the next phase. Examples of evaluation questions and criteria used in
this initial opportunity screening process are shown in Figures 12.3 and 12.4.

- What is the product concept?
- Who are the main customer groups?
- Who is the end user?
- What is the expected function of the product?
- What customer need does it fill?
- What other products fill this customer need?
- Who are the competitors?
- What are the unique features of the product concept?
- What is the domestic market potential?
- What is the foreign market potential?
- What are projected sales in year one?
- What are projected sales in year five?
- What is the projected gross profit?
- What investment is required?
- Is the technology new?
- What is known about safety?
- What are the safety concerns?
- What would the customer pay for the product?
- What is the patent status or opportunity?
- What is the license status or opportunity?
- What is the projected development time?
- What is the anticipated regulatory pathway?
- Are clinical studies required or likely?

Figure 12.3 Questions to consider when evaluating ideas.

Based on business strategy and philosophy, the following should be determined:

- Targeted customers and end users

- Minimum domestic market potential

- Minimum international market potential

- Minimum annual sales

- Maximum investment

- Minimum acceptable gross profit

- Acceptable risk versus benefit

- Need for technology or application to be proprietary

- Requirement for exclusivity in marketplace

- Acceptable regulatory pathway

- Need for fit with existing competencies

Figure 12.4 Examples of idea evaluation criteria.

The criteria must be established by management or in conjunction with management to assure compatibility with strategic business plans. Not all of the questions will be answerable at this stage, but a sufficient number of key answers will be required to present a convincing recommendation for advancement. If there are too many blanks, more homework should be done. Those ideas that do not pass through the screen can be left in the pool to be reevaluated in the future, passed on to affiliate companies, or discarded.

The output of the discovery phase is a development initiation proposal, which is essentially a petition to take a given promising idea into the next phase of product development. The development initiation proposal should contain enough information from relating the evaluation questions to the evaluation criteria to convince management that the specific idea is worthy of being made into a project and that an investment should be made to proceed. Occasionally, a breathtaking idea or opportunity is unearthed that does not fit in with the defined business strategy, but looks like a real star. In such cases, it is the obligation of the product development organization to make the opportunity known to management. Business plans and direction can be modified if the potential is great enough.

At the conclusion of the discovery phase, management approval to continue constitutes an agreement to commit a defined quantity of human and financial resources to take the new project through the feasibility phase. Here, *management* refers to the level or structure within a given company that retains the authority to approve the required level of resources to proceed. Thus, the narrowing of the product development funnel begins.

PHASE 2—FEASIBILITY

Phase 2 of the product development process begins with the identification of a project team and team leader. The nature, size, structure, and philosophy of a company may dictate who identifies the team, what functions are represented on the team, who selects the team leader, what the role of the leader is in shepherding the project through the various stages of development, and whether the team is self-directed, dedicated, or shared. There is no question, though, that the same cross-functional team—all trained in the product development process and familiar with regulatory requirements—should be involved through all phases of a given project. Use of the title *team leader* sometimes causes envy, friction, lack of buy-in among team members, confusion about responsibility and accountability, and misgivings about who will be rewarded for a successful project or held responsible for failure. A more sociologically neutral term such as *guide, facilitator,* or *steward* may be less inflammatory and thus more effective than *leader.*

Feasibility involves concept testing in terms of market opportunity, customer acceptance, technological readiness, basic proof of principle, materials selection, manufacturability, packaging and sterilization options, stability and probable shelf life, and patent issues. The questions asked of an idea in the discovery phase are reconsidered in greater depth during the feasibility phase. If at all possible, an early prototype or mock-up should be evaluated to demonstrate the reality of efficacy, although it is sometimes necessary to base the initial assumptions of safety and/or effectiveness on theory. Now is the time to clearly articulate the product concept and design goal.

During this phase, the testing plan is determined, the desired promotional claims for marketing are defined, the regulatory strategy is set, and a detailed budget reflecting the investment necessary to take the project through to completion is prepared. In other words, the future path of the project is defined. With the availability of a variety of project management software packages, it is nearly inconceivable to think of engaging in product development without computerized assistance. The significant steps in the product development phases that follow feasibility are subject to design controls as required by the FDA and by international quality and regulatory organizations. The software packages can generate a project plan that will form the basis of the design controls system.

At the conclusion of the feasibility phase, the project team determines the likelihood of successful execution of the project and makes a recommendation, detailed in a development continuation proposal to the design review committee, which will be the group responsible for design review as required by design controls regulations.

The original management group responsible for approving the development initiation proposal, if different from the design review committee, may elect to have veto power based on business reasons that transcend the reasons that the project team will present to either continue with a project or to kill it. The product development funnel is further narrowed.

If a project receives approval to be taken into Phase 3 (optimization), a project contract between management and the project team is advisable. The project team agrees to develop the product on a time line that is based on real information and that is acceptable to the team and to management. The team understands its obligations and recognizes that reward and recognition—or the absence thereof—depends on adherence of the team to its proposal and the timely attainment of milestones. For its part, management agrees to provide the needed financial, moral, and labor support, and provides the team with the assurance that, during the next phase, the plug will not be pulled on the project—at least not for spurious reasons.

PHASE 3—OPTIMIZATION

Optimization means refining the product design so that the product meets expectations for function, form, and performance. The activities involved in optimization, the results of these activities, the recommendations made by the project team, the reasons for the recommendations, and the results of the design review must be documented.

During the optimization phase, the design is completed and product attributes and product specifications are further defined, refined, and frozen. Therefore, elements important to the user/product interface—that is, human factors—must be explored and addressed. Final packaging and sterilization requirements are identified, and required materials for manufacturing and packaging are procured. The investment in any necessary new machinery, equipment, or tooling is made. Prototypes are fabricated, shelf-life studies are initiated, and all required preclinical safety and efficacy testing is conducted. If clinical testing on human subjects will be required for product approval, an IDE or IND is prepared using the data generated during optimization. Depending on the product, and if the product does not need clinical testing requiring an IDE or IND, it may be possible to prepare and submit documentation for clearance or approval to the FDA at the end of this phase.

Depending on how the tasks and assessments progress during the optimization phase, the project team will either recommend that the project be killed or it will submit an extension of the development continuation proposal to the design review committee. Design review at the end of the optimization phase will ascertain whether the product performance meets product requirements; whether the product meets customer needs; whether cost and price are acceptable; and whether there are any issues with safety, effectiveness, reliability, or ease of use. If a project makes it through optimization, and if the right assessments have been made and documented, the probability of an eventual regulatory approval or clearance is high. The product development funnel has become very narrow and very focused.

PHASE 4—DEMONSTRATION

Demonstration includes pilot-scale manufacturing and validation of the manufacturing process to prove that the product can be made as anticipated. The product made during this phase is evaluated in clinical studies (if clinicals are required) to demonstrate clinical safety and effectiveness when the product is used as intended.

Not every project will go through the demonstration phase; some will move directly from optimization to production. Demonstration is appropriate if it is desirable for a product to be launched from a pilot manufacturing facility—perhaps while a larger facility is being constructed. This phase may also be wise if lengthy clinical studies are required, especially if there is any question regarding the significance of the outcomes of the clinical studies. In this case, investment in additional facilities can be delayed until there is greater certainty of clinical success and regulatory approval. If the product from this phase will be launched or evaluated in clinical studies, the manufacturing process must meet GMP requirements and the pilot-scale product must be validated to ensure that it meets specifications and all safety and efficacy requirements. If the required regulatory submissions were not made during Phase 3 (optimization), they are prepared and forwarded to the FDA.

If all goes well with the demonstration phase, the project team will probably recommend taking the project into the next phase. The project plans may call for a launch from pilot facilities, in which case the project will move to Phase 6 (launch and follow-through), or to Phase 5 (production) and Phase 6 simultaneously. In any case, an extension of the development continuation proposal will again be presented to the design review committee.

PHASE 5—PRODUCTION

Production is the final scaled-up manufacturing stage for commercial production of the product. The manufacturing process, equipment, and facilities must be validated and must comply with GMP regulations. The product from the production phase must be evaluated to assure that it meets specifications and will be safe and efficacious in use. If regulatory approval or clearance is in hand, the design review committee will be asked to approve launch of the product.

PHASE 6—LAUNCH AND FOLLOW-THROUGH

While many of the individuals involved in the product development process may regard their work as being completed, it is not so. The fruits of their labor are visible and tangible evidence of a successful development plan, but the success of the product is still at risk. Clearly, team members from marketing and sales will be especially active. But operations and quality assurance team members must monitor the manufacturing process and the product being produced, and R&D team members should provide support to the field through educational programs and by supplying answers to customers' technical or medical questions. The FDA may require post-marketing surveillance of certain products as a condition of their remaining on the market. This requires substantial regulatory and medical or clinical affairs activity.

There is, of course, no guarantee that a project emerging from the process described will live up to its expectations and be immune to defects, adverse reactions, or recalls. But with a clever and dedicated product development organization, a supportive and enthusiastic management structure, and diligent adherence to the quality-based project plans and teamwork, the new project has an excellent chance to be a winner.

13

Components of Product Development Planning
Development Portfolio Management

More is in vain when less will sustain.

—Attributed to William of Ockham (paraphrased)

Can we ever have too much of a good thing?

—Miguel de Cervantes

When investing in the stock market to make money over a long period of time, it is customary to maintain a stock portfolio. The portfolio may have a mix of growth and income investments, blue-chip and start-up stocks, and so forth. The balance of the investments in the portfolio is tailored to reflect the immediate needs as well as the future financial goals of the particular investor. Similarly, companies maintain a product portfolio, generally consisting of a mix of different types of products—some are old standbys with strong name-identity value, some are modifications or new applications of the traditional products, and some are new to the company or perhaps even to the marketplace. The mix of product categories reflects the business position of the company, as well as its goals. Companies specializing in products with short lifecycles—those easily and quickly obsolesced by competitive activity or rapidly changing customer needs—require a higher ratio of new products in the product portfolio than companies whose products have relatively long average lifecycles. Maintaining the proper product mix in a product portfolio helps a company minimize long-term risk.

In a parallel fashion, a successful product development organization must maintain a portfolio of development projects. Development portfolio management is an integral component of product development planning (see Figure 13.1). Development portfolio management maximizes control and minimizes risk in keeping a company's strategy for new products compatible with its business needs, objectives, and resources. It can ensure a continual flow of promising ideas into the product development funnel, provide guidelines for converting ideas into projects, track and monitor progress of active projects, and define milestones for continuing projects versus killing projects as they progress through the development funnel. Thus, managing the development portfolio provides a link between opportunities, development projects, new products, and business strategy.

Development portfolio management requires: (1) establishing a model for portfolio assessment or analysis; (2) the existence of and adherence to a defined product development process; and (3) integration with formal technology assessment activities.

Portfolio assessment will reveal the existent technical strategy of the company and measure how well that strategy is integrated with the business. Implementing a defined product development process will provide the foundation for a company to be successful in developing projects in the portfolio and bringing new products to market. A formal technology assessment program will assure that the mid- to long-range technical strategy is aligned with the business strategy. These three elements should be regarded as

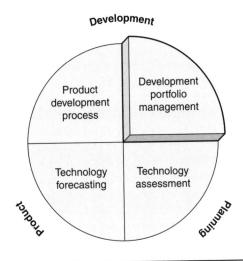

Figure 13.1 Development portfolio management is an integral component of product development planning.

interdependent and inextricable from development and technology management in product development planning.

The purpose of product development portfolio assessment is to:

- Identify development programs and activities.

- Categorize development programs and activities.

- Guide the development programs.

- Provide a fit and value framework for evaluating new ideas/ new project opportunities.

- Guide acquisition, licensing, and divestiture activities.

- Provide measurements that allow comparisons and benchmarking.

- Evaluate the fit of the development programs and activities with the overall technology and business strategies of the company.

There are many models used in business for assessing product or project portfolios. A product development organization may either adapt one of the existing models to product development activities or create a new customized model.

Portfolio assessment captures the position of a given project relative to other projects in the overall context of the business strategy. Every resource-requiring product development project or opportunity should go into the portfolio. Each project is examined in terms of a variety of attributes and risks. The examination criteria mesh with those used to evaluate new ideas and to determine whether a project is allowed to advance through the development funnel, as presented earlier in this book. We see now that there is an apparent "chicken or egg" conundrum. Which comes first—a model for portfolio assessment or a product development process? Since they can't spring into existence simultaneously and fully formed, the most empirical and practical approach would be to define a product development process first. The experience gained with applying discriminatory criteria to individual projects as they wend their way through the development phases (discovery, feasibility, optimization, demonstration, production, launch, and follow-through) will bring focus and relevance to elements of portfolio assessment.

The framework used to assess ideas, projects, new-to-the-company product opportunities, and future new product possibilities should be based on a group of essential core qualities applicable to all four components of product development planning. Some examples of core qualities are given in Table 13.1. This type of review may be adapted to provide information that is primarily qualitative, semi-quantitative, or highly quantitative. Depending

Table 13.1 Framework for basic assessment of ideas, projects, and future opportunities.

Issue	Status	
Customer/market need	Now met	Unmet
Market opportunity	Small	Large
Market growth	Low	High
Fit with business strategy	Poor	Good
Profitability	Low	High
Profit impact on company	Small	Large
Competition	Strong	Weak
Patent position/exclusivity	Weak	Strong
Time to commercialize	Long	Short
Company technological capability	New	Existing
Regulatory obstacles	Difficult	Less difficult
Investment required	High	Low

on the component of product development planning to which the basic evaluation scheme will be applied, certain issues will become more or less important, and different assessment issues may be added to or deleted from the scheme. It is important to identify the most important issues and to consider them in a way that will allow information from one stage of product development planning to flow smoothly into another stage. Before engaging in any type of assessment, it is critical to first clarify the customer and the end user, and the nature of the clinical need that is expected to be addressed.

Portfolio assessment requires some system of data collection, matrices, and measurements. The approach can range from very straightforward and Spartan to enormously complex and draconian. There is no intrinsically right or wrong way to do it. If a product development organization has the opportunity and flexibility to define its own model, as opposed perhaps to using a corporate model, the most important elements would be understandability, ease of use, meaningfulness of data, and consistency of application. These qualities are very specific to particular businesses, cultures, and organizational structures and, consequently, work best when they are at least somewhat customized. Portfolio analysis is not a one-size-fits-all process.

A key to portfolio assessment is mapping. Mapping is a tool in which individual components of some collection—such as products or projects—are evaluated according to various sets of characteristics. Mapping allows a visual presentation of relationships among projects, and between projects and the evaluation criteria. There is no limit to the nature and number of qualities that may be evaluated, so selectivity must be based on the objectives and strategy of the company and the product development organization. Project information, for example, can be presented in ways that range from primarily qualitative to highly quantitative. However, important elements to capture in terms of project evaluation include:

- Degree of correlation of each project with short-, mid-, and long-range business strategy

- Customer need/market need

- Cost to complete development and launch

- Category of project

- Developmental stage of project (its location in the funnel)

- New product launch year

- Projected sales

- Resource requirements

- Technical feasibility

- Projected profit

Data and information can be arrayed in any manner that provides an informative visual presentation, including bar graphs, line graphs, pie charts, and so on. For the purpose of illustration, consider a very simplified boilerplate matrix that classifies attributes into two categories along each axis, as shown generically in Figure 13.2. The attributes evaluated reflect anything relevant to the business, the business strategy, and to established regulatory and quality requirements. Examples would generally include reference to customers, markets, technological feasibility, costs, time to commercialize, and so on. In other words, we would examine the core features in the evaluation framework shown in Table 13.1, with certain modifications particularly applicable to portfolio analysis (see Table 13.2). In this simple model, the status of each attribute is categorized into one of two complementary extremes, such as low/high, old/new, same/different, weak/strong. Of course, the maps that are generated must then be interpreted. Depending on the interpretation, an action plan can be defined and implemented. Figure 13.3 shows an example of a possible interpretation based on quadrant location, using an analogy to a poker game.

A look at how a new product development organization for a fictitious company might map projects should further illustrate the concept of mapping. One type of map that is useful in classifying projects according to

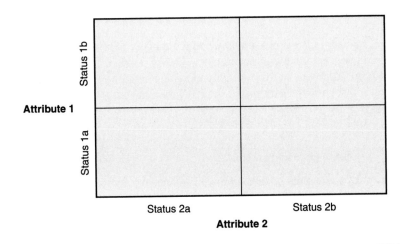

Figure 13.2 A simple generic portfolio map matrix.

Table 13.2 Additional characteristics for project mapping.

Attributes	Status Pairs	
	(a)	(b)
Sales (Year 1, Year 5, etc.)	Old	New
Technological Risks	Same	Different
Manufacturability	Yes	No
Ease-of-Use	Weak	Strong
Outcomes Advantages	Easy	Difficult
Global Opportunities	Clear	Unclear
Return on Investment	Certain	Uncertain
Fit with Core Competencies	Small	Large
Stage of Development	Early	Late
Requirement for New Process Development	Low	High
Competitive Advantage		
Product Life Span		
Gross Profit		
Financial Risk		
Probability of On-Time Development		
Probability of Successful Development		
Availability of Required Resources		

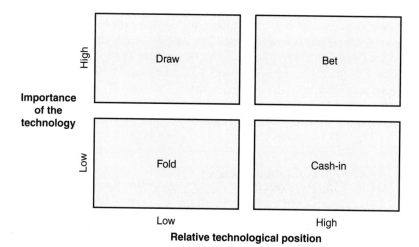

The four quadrants are described as follows:

- **Bet.** The company is in a technologically excellent position in a business segment where that technology is important: objectives should be to sustain and increase competitive advantage. This is the business where one must commit oneself to the newest equipment.

- **Draw.** The company is in a borderline position. One needs to make two decisions: either bet against the competition and invest to attain a leadership position, or develop a plan to disengage from, or even abandon, that technology and invest in more lucrative areas.

- **Cash-in.** The company is in a technologically strong position, but the technology where it excels is not really important in marketplace terms. This situation occurs most often in a rapidly changing industry, such as electronics or engineered plastics, where existing technology is continually being supplanted by new techniques. Technologies underlying aging product families (frequently a company's original product lines) tend to lie in this quadrant too.

- **Fold.** The company is technologically weak in an unimportant field. If heavy investment has taken place, this money may have to be considered to be sunk costs. If not, then a financial redeployment strategy is essential (and the sooner the better).

Figure 13.3   An example of a technology portfolio matrix.

Source: Arie P. Nagel, "A Framework for Technology Strategy" in *Product Development,* edited by Margaret Bruce and Wim G. Biemans (Chichester: John Wiley & Sons, 1995): 69. Copyright © 1995 by John Wiley & Sons, Ltd. Reprinted by permission of John Wiley & Sons, Ltd.

new product categories plots the market addressed with regard to the company (current versus new) against the technology requirement with regard to the company (current versus new) (see Figure 13.4). Assume, for the sake of the example, that a hypothetical company has six development projects, each represented by a different letter: A through F.

Figure 13.5 shows how these projects sort out when mapped to reflect the market addressed versus the technology requirement. Figure 13.5 shows

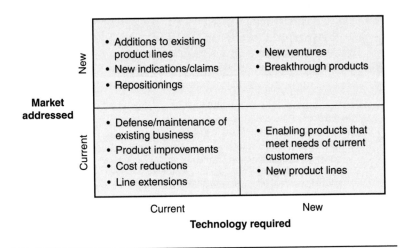

Figure 13.4 Portfolio map matrix showing types of projects.

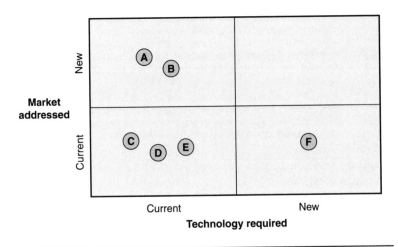

Figure 13.5 A project map for a fictitious company: is it good or bad?

a clustering of projects addressing the fictitious company's current market and that can be accomplished with the company's current technology. There are no projects that address a different market and that also involve a technology that the company does not currently have. What the map shows, then, is that half of the projects in the development portfolio of the company relate to doing little things with existing products—perhaps size changes, repackaging, or cost-improvement efforts. One-third of the projects involve relying on the current technology to somehow address a different market—perhaps through adding new claims or new indications for use to a current product. The remaining project involves a new technology to address the current market—possibly a licensing arrangement for a previously competitive product. Conspicuously absent are any projects that would expand both the market and the technological capabilities of the company, which could include projects that are, in addition to being new to the company, new to the market or even new to the world.

The next issue that must be considered is whether to interpret this mix of projects as good or not good. To do this, there must be some concept of what would constitute the ideal maps for a given company. Reality would then be compared to the ideal to provide direction to the development strategy. Although there are no one-size-fits-all-companies ideal maps, there is clear reason to avoid projects that fall into a quadrant that encompasses two negative elements, such as small market opportunity coupled with poor fit with business strategies, or something falling into the "Fold" quadrant defined in Figure 13.3.

For some companies, notably those adverse to risk-taking but satisfied with running in a maintenance mode, the assortment of projects seen in Figure 13.5 may be acceptable. Companies interested in extensive and rapid growth, however, would recognize the need to fill the empty quadrant and reassess the wisdom of having a large number of low-risk projects.

The most important purpose, by far, of engaging in the exercise of portfolio assessment is to assure that the product development activities of the company are integrated with the business. Consequently, it is possible to evaluate the meaning of the maps only if they are considered in context with the specific business. This means that development portfolio assessment is not an exercise just for scientists, and it is not an exercise just for marketing people. It must be a cross-functional activity and, at some point, must include individuals with significant management authority and detailed knowledge of where the business wants to go and how much it is willing to invest to get there. It may not be logistically feasible for all product development team members to participate in portfolio assessment, but a significant number of those participating in portfolio assessment should be involved in product development.

Individuals involved with portfolio analysis must be able to make recommendations and decisions within the context of the business strategy. During review of the projects and portfolio, decisions will have to be made whether to continue or discontinue each project. The fit of each project with requirements for projected sales potential, business compatibility, technological feasibility, and time and resource requirements, for example, must be constantly challenged.

With a few exceptions, there is no particular quadrant within a given map in which a company must feel obligated to play, nor one from which it is mandatory to stay away. The play or stay away decision depends on where the company envisions itself at present and in the future. Placing projects in a quadrant that reflects high investment and low return might be an obvious situation for company ABC to avoid, but might make sense for company XYZ if it would provide dominance or control of a market in which XYZ is already a player.

Another thing to bear in mind is that, for portfolio assessment to be useful, it must be an ongoing exercise. Development portfolios with many projects generally require more frequent analysis and review than portfolios with fewer projects. The frequency of review should also reflect the vibrancy or conversely the torpor of the company, as well as the number of projects in the portfolio. Business strategies evolve and change. Six months after company XYZ has committed to a high investment/low return project in order to gain market dominance, the controlling management of XYZ may decide to exit that market entirely. Project continuance and resource allocation would obviously have to be readdressed, and the configuration of the portfolio would be altered.

Similarly, there can be changes in the competitive environment that affect the value of a particular project, regardless of its position on the maps. If ABC gets clearance or approval from the FDA to introduce a new product, for example, it can suddenly become very important for ABC to prioritize a similar project that doesn't look particularly attractive based on most attributes, but which can be developed in a very short time and provide stronger name recognition for ABC in that market. Meanwhile, company XYZ, which also had been nurturing a similar project, might decide to kill the project, since its strategy does not include being a me-too player in that market. If, on the other hand, ABC had failed to gain FDA clearance or approval, XYZ might well have accelerated the project, in hopes of now being the first to market.

In addition to the right-for-the-company categorical mix of projects, mapping should include presentations of the stage of development of each project and an indication of when the resulting new product will be launched. Remember, the time remaining before launch is not necessarily reflected by the developmental stage of a project. A pharmaceutical or Class III device requiring new clinical trials may be in a relatively advanced (late) stage of development, but still require years before product launch. By comparison, a line extension for a Class I or Class II device might be in the earliest developmental stage, with an idea approved but without any additional follow-up—yet this early-stage project could lead to a product launch in far less than a year. It is important to identify gaps in timing, as well as in project type. One can become very creative in combining representations of three, four, or more product characteristics in one map. Use of color and the depiction of individual projects in different shapes and sizes to reflect such things as developmental stage and sales potential are tricks that can be used.

Some organizations, whether they use primarily qualitative or highly quantitative maps and matrices, assign weight to the factors being considered in portfolio assessment, according to a perceived importance to the business. Since it is clear that, in the final analysis, subjective reaction and good technical and business judgment are the most important tools in making decisions about projects, weighting can be problematic. It is not always possible to describe and assign weight to some of the softer, fuzzier reasons that a project may be important. A product development organization that applies weighting to yield a score that is supposed to reflect the priority/ desirability/value/urgency of a project will inevitably find itself at times at odds with the score and rank of a project and what the organization intuitively knows is the real importance of, or danger of, a project. This, then, generally leads to going back to redo the numbers, modifying the objective score of a project so that it more closely reflects what the company plans to do with it anyway.

Occasionally, too, a product development organization will find itself in the grasp of immediate management so slavishly enamored of strict adherence to a process that judgment and intuitiveness are subjugated to the absolute output of that process. Important opportunities are likely to be passed up or dismissed in favor of higher-scoring but less worthy endeavors. This is especially likely in portfolio assessment if weighting is used.

By the way, beware of becoming an individual to whom a process is an end unto itself. A process should be a servant, not a master.

A very common and very dangerous tendency is for an organization to include too many projects in its development portfolio, most often in a misguided attempt to please or impress management. One way to avoid the problem is to attain management buy-in and understanding of product development planning and of the stages and requirements of the product development process.

It's easy to understand why the company president bristles when informed by the product development organization that what, at first blush, appears to be a simple and straightforward project to develop a new product will require three times the resources and five times the time to get to launch than he or she thinks it should. There are always a plethora of examples that the president can give of other companies that can launch products in a fraction of the time. In reality, the other company's new products might not really be that similar in terms of, for example, clinical and regulatory requirements. But the cause of underproductivity in a product development organization can often be traced to lack of understanding of product development—within management ranks and within the product development group itself. It is clear that, if the product development organization understands and engages in the practices of a sound product development planning system, it will be better equipped to educate management. If management, in turn, grasps the basic concepts and is willing to be educated as to which elements of development are quality and regulatory requirements and which cannot be considered optional, management support is much more likely.

Having too many projects in relation to available resources with the proper and necessary skills means that development work will be impaired and unfocused. Efforts will become disjointed and disorganized as people rush from project to project, putting out fires on some while losing momentum on others. Portfolio management offers the opportunity to apply some of the principles of Henry David Thoreau in the workplace. No, not civil disobedience, although that can sometimes be the net result of failure to institute the other principle. The relevant principle is, of course, simplification. If portfolio assessment reveals that there are more projects than appropriate people to work on them, actions must be triggered or else the exercise of portfolio assessment should be discontinued. If the discipline to simplify and to kill projects is lacking, the portfolio will just keep filling up with more and more projects—all of which seem valuable and desirable. Everyone's time will be spent analyzing projects, filling out data forms, constructing maps, and justifying the necessity of including all of these projects for the success of the company. Financial resources will be drained by trying to support or breathe life into projects that no longer merit investment. Eventually, nothing at all will actually get developed.

KILLING A PROJECT

Don't be afraid to kill a project. If the criteria for killing a project are well thought-out and accepted by everyone (or at least by a sound majority) of those involved in the portfolio assessment activity, the decision to kill a project is overwhelmingly likely to be the right decision.

It can be extremely difficult to pull the plug on a development project. There is a tendency to regard the action as an admission of personal or group inadequacy or defeat. Sometimes individuals become so emotionally attached to a project that letting go causes psychological distress. At times, it seems more palatable to kill the project manager than to kill the project. Occasionally, though, people involved with a project that is just not working out will become demoralized, recognizing that the project is hopeless but uncertain of how to convey the agony to decision makers. For them, killing the project would bring a sense of relief and an end to pain.

As shown in Figure 13.6, discontinuing a project should be seriously considered if the criteria for selecting the project no longer apply to a project; if troubling and significant but unforeseen changes in the competitive, regulatory, or medical environment occur; if access to or availability of raw materials becomes seriously compromised; if milestones have not been met and cannot be met in the future; or if common sense and good judgment just cry out that the project is hopeless.

Some healthcare companies hold celebratory parties when a project is killed, and others stage mock funerals. Unless an overwhelmingly compelling reason exists—for example, you still have three years development time ahead of you on the project, but yesterday three competitors announced the launch of new products that do the same thing better, more safely, and more economically than your planned product—rather than bury the project, put the idea in the back of the closet. Every now and then, take it out, shake it out, dust it off, and reexamine it. Shifts in company mission, vision, customer needs, market, or technologies might provide an opportunity to resurrect the project in a new environment that would enhance its success.

- The market opportunity no longer exists.
- A change in business strategy results in poor fit.
- The regulatory environment becomes very unfavorable.
- Raw materials are no longer readily available.
- Required technological capabilities are unattainable.
- Milestones cannot be met.
- The entire team agrees that the project is hopeless.

Figure 13.6 Signs that a project should be killed.

Portfolio management is a method of making sure that product development activities will support business objectives. The proper mix of development projects will provide a steady stream of new product introductions and assure that the products being developed are the right products.

14

Components of Product Development Planning
Technology Assessment

Fooling around with alternating currents is just a waste of time. Nobody will use it, ever. It's too dangerous.

—Thomas Alva Edison

The general public has long been divided into two parts: those who think science can do anything, and those who are afraid it will.

—Dixy Lee Ray

In a number of the preceding chapters, the concept of technology assessment has been mentioned. Technology assessment is one of the key elements in the integrated approach to product development encompassed in product development planning (see Figure 14.1). The objective of technology assessment is to identify available technologies that have the greatest fit with the business strategy and market need, as well as a high probability of technical success (see Figure 14.2).

Product development planning allows the formation of a technology strategy by linking an ongoing assessment of existing, new, emerging, and embryonic technologies with the process of technology forecasting as a vision of the future. The technology strategy, in turn, forms the foundation for a portfolio of new potential product development projects. Management of the development portfolio depends upon successful implementation of a defined product development process.

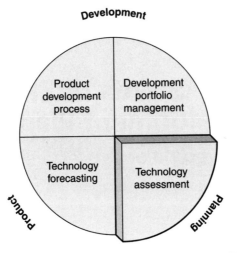

Figure 14.1 Technology assessment is an integral component of product development planning.

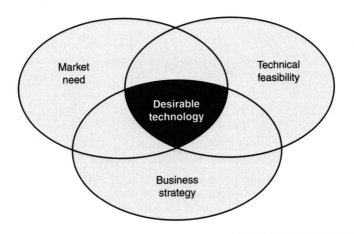

Figure 14.2 Considerations in technology assessment.

Technology assessment means identifying and evaluating existing, new, emerging, and embryonic technologies. It incorporates critical factors— scientific, clinical, regulatory, legal, market-related, social, political, and ethical—that can influence the success, profitability, and lifecycle of a technology. Technology assessment has its most pronounced influence on the near- to mid-term planning for new product development.

Healthcare product development requires information from the market to be meshed with scientific opportunities in order to yield a viable, desirable new product. The scientific opportunities may exist or be presented in a plethora of forms, including:

- Basic technological offerings from start-up companies

- University-based applied research programs

- Patents and scientific literature

- New product ideas being developed by other companies

- Product suggestions from customers

- New products already developed but not yet commercialized

- Marketing and licensing opportunities

- Acquisition targets

These opportunities often enter an organization through research or product development groups, through marketing, or through the business development department of a company. Business development groups may constitute the most common contact from outside companies with an idea, technology, or product to sell.

One typical scenario is for someone from business development of a small company to contact someone in business development of another, larger company. The small company has a technology about which it wants to make a presentation, in hopes of enticing the larger company to provide financial support to continue development work. In exchange, the smaller company will try to negotiate an agreement allowing certain rights related to any future product sales to the larger company. The business development people from the two companies make arrangements to meet to review the idea. From this point on, things all too frequently begin to go astray. For example, while the company with the idea to sell may have a scientific person provide a simplified technical overview, the audience often consists of nonscientist business development personnel and perhaps an assorted financial or operations individual. The audience takes on good faith the always outstanding safety and performance information presented by the company with the idea. Since audience members are unable or unprepared to ask any relevant and probing questions related to scientific data or regulatory issues, serious potential problems will be overlooked at the onset. Furthermore, since the company receiving the information has no one present with the appropriate grasp of the market or with the relevant and probing questions related to the marketplace or to users, the need or utility of the technology or resulting product will not be confirmed at the onset.

It is clear that the decision-making process with regard to action on the idea will be compromised in this case. If they are too gullible, the decision makers may make a financial commitment to developing a new product for which there is inadequate market need or that has virtually no probability of gaining regulatory approval or clearance. If they are too cynical, the decision makers may believe that the potential is unrealistically overinflated and overhyped and pass up a real gem.

There are other common versions of this scenario, many of which are flawed because the people with the appropriate skills and knowledge bases are excluded from such meetings. Marketing personnel may be present, but product development personnel absent, or the converse might be the case. The point is that when all of the necessary knowledge is not available to business development efforts that involve assessing existing, new, emerging, or embryonic technology, time, money, and effort are wasted. Perhaps worse, really good opportunities may be lost. Some of the critical skills that come into play in informed technology assessment efforts are given in Figure 14.3. When healthcare products are involved, it makes a great deal of sense to have scientifically trained, dedicated staff members involved in technology assessment.

When assessing the value of new technological opportunities, it is critical to clarify the customer and the end user, and the magnitude and nature of the clinical need that is expected to be addressed. If there are other technologies in place for use in the same or similar medical conditions, some clear advantages *that will be important to customers* must exist. If there are, for example, presumed advantages in terms of safety, clinical effectiveness, usability, outcomes, or cost, it is important to establish that the differences are qualitatively and quantitatively sufficient to persuade adoption of the resulting new product. One cannot simply assume what customers' reactions would be (much less the FDA's). The information must come from the targeted customer. Don't forget nondomestic customers. In reflecting on the potential for global new product introductions, any positive or negative cultural issues must be examined.

Marketing

- Knowledge of targeted market
- Understanding of targeted customers and users
- Understanding of promotional opportunities and limitations
- Access to information regarding market size, number of procedures, and so on, to establish need
- Familiarity with existing alternatives and competitors, if any
- Cost, pricing, coverage, and reimbursement issues

Scientific

- Ability to assess significance of medical need
- Understanding completeness and validity of safety data
- Understanding completeness and validity of preclinical efficacy studies
- Ability to evaluate any completed or ongoing clinical studies
- Ability to recognize technical "red flags"
- Grasp of feasibility of successful development
- Knowledge of current scientific, health, and medical issues
- Access to IP evaluation resources

Regulatory

- Ability to determine probable required regulatory pathway
- Knowledge of current relevant regulatory issues
- Understanding of testing and manufacturing requirements
- Access to product- or technology-related regulatory history
- Grasp of registration and review time requirements
- Grasp of probability of regulatory success
- Experience in communicating/negotiating with FDA

Figure 14.3 Examples of critical skills and knowledge base for informed technology assessment.

There may be opportunities for access to a new technology that could replace an existing product that already satisfactorily meets current customer needs. The new technology may be attractive because it offers certain advantages to the manufacturer—perhaps in terms of cost, availability of materials, or greater manufacturing control. In such cases, unless the product changes are completely invisible to the customer, it is once again critical to talk to and listen to the customer before switching to the new technology. There have been countless market failures in the healthcare field resulting from companies neglecting to obtain customer reactions to product concepts or product prototypes before introducing the product.

New technologies can bring added future value to a company if they have the potential of serving as a platform for the future development of a variety of new product derivatives. If an opportunity can become a new company core technology, the life span—and hence the overall value—of the technology can be increased. Similarly, if a licensing agreement to a patented technology is the opportunity being pursued, guaranteed exclusivity along with the proprietary nature of the product technology can serve as formidable barriers to competitive product entries.

Technology readiness and novelty are important considerations. Depending on the scale of development of the technology—bench top, breadboard prototype, pilot, in clinical evaluation, fully manufactured—different questions about manufacturability scale-up problems, or limitations will become relevant. Novelty and readiness, in conjunction with competitive development activities, can influence the likelihood of premature obsolescence because of other new or emerging technologies. When implementing product development planning, it is crucial to integrate the key requirements pertaining to business strategy, customers, and product attributes into the processes of product development, portfolio analysis, and technology assessment. If the lists of example questions given in this book for each of these components seem redundant, it is because they are purposefully redundant. Identifying the most important considerations, phrasing questions that will give information about those considerations, and consistently analyzing and interpreting that information will ensure proper focus and alignment of product development planning with business objectives. Core issues must be addressed in all key components of product development planning, yet each component will bring in its own new interests and objectives. In keeping with the goal of a unified framework for assessment of new ideas, projects, products, and opportunities, Table 14.1 presents the basic scheme for evaluation, and Figure 14.4 gives some additional topics for questions that might typically be relevant to healthcare technology assessment.

Table 14.1 Framework for basic assessment of ideas, projects, and future opportunities.

Issue	Status	
Customer/market need	Now met	Unmet
Market opportunity	Small	Large
Market growth	Low	High
Fit with business strategy	Poor	Good
Profitability	Low	High
Profit impact on company	Small	Large
Competition	Strong	Weak
Patent position/exclusivity	Weak	Strong
Time to commercialize	Long	Short
Company technological capability	New	Existing
Regulatory obstacles	Difficult	Less difficult
Investment required	High	Low

- Developmental stage
- Existing regulatory approval/clearance
- Fit with mid- to long-term business strategy
- Management support
- Outcomes advantages
- Other competitive advantages
- Business risk
- Technical feasibility
- Readiness of technology
- Knowledge of/access to customers
- Positive medical, social, cultural, legal, or ethical issues
- Negative medical, social, cultural, legal, or ethical issues
- Availability of required resources
- Return on investment

Figure 14.4 Additional issues relevant to technology assessment. *continued*

continued

- Gross profit
- Potential as platform technology
- Global applicability
- Technology life span/vulnerability to obsolescence

Figure 14.4 Additional issues relevant to technology assessment.

15

Components of Product Development Planning

Technology Forecasting

Prediction is very difficult, especially about the future.

—Attributed to Niels Bohr

The Future . . . something which everyone reaches at the rate of sixty minutes an hour.

—C. S. Lewis

It may seem an elusive goal in these somewhat chaotic and unpredictable times, but technology forecasting is about anticipating the future. Anticipating the future allows the formation of a suitable and planned technology strategy. It also alerts a business organization to the possible need for a shift or an evolution in its business strategy. Be assured, a company involved in medical products that is not involved in technology forecasting will eventually lose its competitive edge. As an integral component of product development planning, technology forecasting is essential to the survival and growth of healthcare companies in an ever-changing environment (see Figure 15.1). The linkage of technology forecasting with technology assessment allows a technology strategy to be defined. The technology strategy, in turn, forms the foundation for filling the product development funnel, and hence the development portfolio, with new project opportunities.

You will notice that the operative word with regard to the future is *anticipating,* not *predicting.* In trying to visualize the course of scientific and

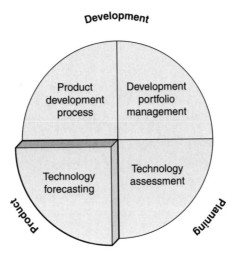

Figure 15.1 Technology forecasting is an integral component of product development planning.

technological advances, it is not possible to consider four key elements that would actually allow an informed prediction to be made: (1) serendipity, (2) the quirkiness and unpredictability of Mother Nature, (3) the destructive capabilities of the human race, and (4) the rate of scientific and technological discoveries and advances—even of those that we're quite certain are on the horizon. Consider the following:

- It took 122 years to issue the first million U.S. patents; 24 years to issue the second million; and eight years to issue the one million patents spanning the fifth and sixth million.

- It took centuries to identify the cause of cholera, two years to identify the cause of AIDS, and about two weeks to identify the cause of severe acute respiratory syndrome (SARS).

For this reason, technology forecasting, which is generally directed at scenarios more than five years in the future, should not strive for precision in terms of events or time lines.

Technology forecasting requires closer attention to pure scientific activity than is required by other elements of product development planning. This is because scientific discovery and technology are interdependent and inextricable (see Figure 15.2). As new scientific phenomena

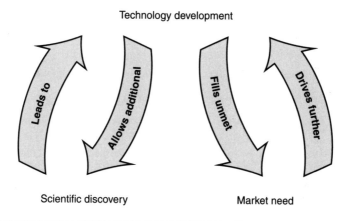

Figure 15.2   The relationship between science, technology, and market.

are uncovered, techniques are created to address or approach resulting scientific questions, which results in additional new information and discovery. The new techniques, in turn, can exploit this new information by applying it to other scientific (or medical) needs or problems. This exercise results both in driving further technology development to improve outcomes, and in the revelation of more scientific information through data generation (which leads to more technological advances, and so on, *ad infinitum*).

As an example, consider the ongoing scientific examination entailed in the human genome project. As the mapping of the human genome proceeds, we have witnessed the new opportunities for genetic therapy in which normal, functioning copies of abnormal genes are introduced into the patient to do the work that the abnormal version of the genes are incapable of doing. We have also been witness to the unpredictable and sometimes disastrous consequences of gene therapy. In just a few years of observation of the likely direction of gene mapping, entrepreneurs have developed or are developing:

- Diagnostic procedures and the associated chemistries, disposables, hardware, and software

- Therapies to prevent or postpone the onset of symptoms associated with diagnosed genetic predispositions

- Therapies to restore deficiencies resulting from genetic disorders

- Vehicles and devices for the delivery of therapeutic treatments

- Improved (simplified, miniaturized, more rapid) devices and instrumentation to isolate and amplify genetic sequences for therapeutic purposes

- Improved instrumentation and devices for forensic genetic analysis

- Patient-specific courses of treatment based on allelic profiles

Further consideration of each of these points, in turn, can provide more opportunity for speculation and visualization of products, in an endless cascade of ideas and applications. Will restorative therapies be conventional drugs? Recombinant enzymes or hormones? Agonists or antagonists of proteins? Antisense molecules? Nucleic acids or cells sourced from the patient? You get the idea.

In imagining the future, a product development organization will require from management an indication of the scope that this visionary process may encompass. To end up with a useful output, there must be some indication of how far and in what direction from the current company mission one can stray in technology forecasting. An open mind is essential in considering the possibilities of scientific and technological advances, while discipline and focus are necessary to stay in sync with the management view of the future company. If there is an absolute, irrevocable proscription against ever becoming a drug company, for example, attention could be given to how the new science might affect diagnostic and surgical procedures, the need for new polymers or other materials, use of disposable or consumable supplies, requirements for specialized instruments and equipment, and so forth. The rapid growth in development and approval of combination products is indicative of some medical product companies' willingness to expand beyond their historically traditional missions.

Like other steps in product development planning, technology forecasting is best served by cross-functional participants. Information for technology forecasting can come from a number of sources, including but not limited to:

- Professional conferences

- Scientific literature

- Patent literature

- Market research

- University alliances

- Customers

- Competitive intelligence networks

- FDA activity and publications

- EPA activity and publications

- National Institutes of Health activity and publications

- Centers for Disease Control and Prevention activity and publications

- Emerging public health issues.

These sources are similar to those from which new product ideas are identified or generated. This is not surprising if you think of technology forecasting as providing the basis for new product ideas with the more distant future in mind.

While brainstorming and no-holds-barred creativity sessions have their place in technology forecasting, study and extrapolation of trends is very important. Often in the process of technology forecasting, the view is so firmly fixed on the future that the starting point is the present, or possibly even the future. In fact, the starting point for anticipating the future should be the past. An analysis of trends shows how we got to the present and identifies the drivers, obstacles, and success of the outcomes.

There are scientific, technological, political, legal, social, economic, cultural, ethical, and environmental trends that themselves have affected healthcare trends and that have defined the current state of affairs. An understanding of each contributor and an educated, informed extrapolation based on both historical and emerging data will help to maximize the probability of accuracy in the vision of the future. Forecasts that are supported by converging trends will generally be more viable and associated with more significant opportunities. As an example, consider the factors that have been identified as contributing to the emergence of new diseases in humans, such as AIDS, Ebola, SARS, and monkeypox, to the reemergence of previously controlled diseases, such as tuberculosis, and to the disturbing increase in occurrence of antibiotic-resistant pathogens (see Figure 15.3). By looking back in time, epidemiologists are now better prepared to see ahead and to anticipate the possibility of new diseases arising in certain situations. Technology forecasting in the field of infection control would rely on analysis of the same contributing factors to anticipate the future and to develop new product strategies to deal with the anticipated future.

Sometimes the voices of scientists—especially those not espousing popular beliefs—are ignored in the process of technology forecasting. The case of duodenal ulcer treatment is an example. For generations, ulcers were managed by dubious dietary therapies and recommendations to avoid stress, then by antacids, and in severe cases by surgery. Then began the era

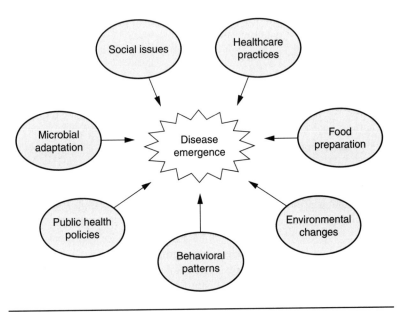

Figure 15.3 Factors contributing to the emergence of new diseases and the reemergence of previously controlled diseases.

of gastric acid secretion inhibition by histamine H2-receptor antagonists. These drugs became the top-selling pharmaceuticals and are now available over the counter. Another class of antisecretory drugs, the proton pump inhibitors, followed. Not unexpectedly, the indication for surgical intervention for ulcers drastically decreased. In the background, though, was a researcher who doggedly believed that ulcers were caused by bacteria. Though pharmaceutical manufacturers resisted the message, the evidence could not be ignored forever. In 1996, the FDA approved the first antibiotic treatment for ulcers.[51] Whether or not the entire evolution from palliative to surgical to suppressive to antiinfective management of duodenal ulcers could have been forecast, the timing of the most recent phase certainly could have been different had greater attention been paid to basic scientific research.

Political agendas can impede the progress of research and the development of new medical products. Whether from deliberate denial or from self-delusional denial, the failure of certain governments to recognize either the existence or implications of, for example, AIDS, variant CJD, or SARS, delayed the quests for diagnostics and therapies.

Analyzing trends and following up with technology strategies based on these analyses can create new sets of problems, or, as product development people prefer to say, opportunities. Since the 1980s, technology forecasting (and resultant product development efforts) have increasingly followed a shift from interest in acute illnesses to addressing needs associated with chronic and long-term conditions. There are a variety of reasons for this emphasis, ranging from lack of glamour and complacency with the adequacy of existing products to the pressures of managed care. Although issues of antibiotic resistance have been recognized for many decades, the development of new antibiotics decreased during the past 20 years, and scant attention has been paid to the R&D of new classes of antiinfective agents to which microbes could not become resistant. Alternative therapies for a variety of drug-resistant bacterial species is now desperately needed, but the development projects are few and in the early stages. Taking a cue from this unaddressed need, the biotechnology industry is responding by looking at a different approach—that of using host defenses to fight infectious diseases.[52] The basis of this approach lies in the scientific research on how certain animals (including insects) are able to resist infections even when they sustain injuries in very dirty environments.

The vigilance, observation, and imagination to spot where trends are going, to differentiate between true trends and fads, and to identify the gaps left in the wake of the trends are part and parcel of technology forecasting. It is an exercise that requires simultaneous analysis of numerous issues about science, research institutions, medicine, marketing, and regulatory affairs, in addition to imagination, knowledge, and understanding of the long-term company business strategy. Figure 15.4 lists some of the topics that might be addressed during technology forecasting.

The areas of government-funded research activities in healthcare, and the priorities articulated by the FDA, can foreshadow market need and opportunity. Some of the areas of interest that the FDA has expressed are shown in Figure 15.5.

The deliverable at the conclusion of a technology forecasting session should be an identified strategy to monitor some developments and a recommendation to management (with copious justification, of course) to invest and participate in others. All assumptions should be clearly stated in the forecast, and the time horizons should be clear. The nature and degree of participation in follow-up to technology forecasting exercises will depend on the size, vision, and resources of the company. Usually, alternatives for action will include long-range internal research and/or development, codevelopment partnerships with universities or other public or private research groups, and investment in or acquisition of research-oriented companies.

What do you anticipate/speculate will apply to the following in five years? 10 years? 15 years? 20 years?

- Major challenges in health and medicine
- Vision/mission of the company
- Trends in prevention/diagnosis/treatment/monitoring/cure
- Market potential for these trends
- Compatibility with long-term company vision
- Issues/areas neglected or overlooked if trends are widely pursued
- Opportunities in neglected, overlooked areas
- Targeted customers
- New needs for customers
- Globalization and harmonization of international regulatory and quality requirements
- Technologies that could provide solutions
- Solutions that could be provided by current core/platform technologies
- Availability or sources of enabling technologies
- Groups/institutions working on new relevant technologies
- Healthcare provider/healthcare delivery system restrictions
- Competitors and competitive activity
- Possible regulatory scenarios
- Skills and resource needs to meet the challenges

Figure 15.4 Considerations for technology forecasting.

Although accurate predictions are what we may fantasize about as we engage in technology forecasting, no one should enter into the process expecting to experience an epiphany. The objective of technology forecasting should not be to predict events, developments, or timing with assurance. Rather, it is to encourage unconventional, creative thinking about new products, unfettered by the constraints and limitations of the present.

- Treatments for nerve gases and radiologic agents
- Increasing stockpiles of vaccines of bioweapons
- New vaccines
  - Nucleic vaccines
  - Live attenuated vaccines
  - Combination vaccines
  - Therapeutic vaccines
- New diagnostics for blood and tissue safety
- Cell and gene therapy
- Proteomics and pharmacogenomics
- Regenerative medical products and tissue engineering
- Novel drug delivery

Figure 15.5   Areas of interest at the FDA for the 21st century.

16

More for the Laundry List

Marketing, Patents, Budgets, Games, and Quality

. . . And more, and more, and more.

—Lewis Carroll

Synergy means behavior of whole systems unpredicted by the behavior of their parts.

—R. Buckminster Fuller

PLANNING FOR MARKETING

There are strict regulations regarding advertising and promotion of medical products. When the FDA clears or approves a medical device, drug, or biologic for marketing, the agency will define specific indications for use for that product. The indications for use are based on the total package of information provided to the FDA, particularly on safety and efficacy data. The manufacturer or distributor of the product can advertise and promote the product only for the indicate use(s). It is illegal to promote a medical product for any use other than the FDA-approved indicated uses, that is, it is illegal to engage in off-label promotional activities. Now, the FDA does not regulate the practice of medicine, and it is not illegal for a doctor to use a medical product in an off-label indication. There are certain liability risks for the doctor, and for the manufacturer as well, if the doctor chooses to use the product off-label—but it is legal to do so. Have no doubt about this, though—you cannot promote the product for off-label use. So it is important to establish what marketing claims (indications) are mandatory in the view of the company, what indications are desirable, and what development activities will be required to attempt to achieve the articulated corporate promotional goals.

The promotional objectives, of course, have to be realistic, given the nature, design, and fundamental intention of the product idea. By the time the clinical plan is being formulated for those products requiring clinical trials, it is essential to have this issue resolved. A good clinical plan asks the right questions in the right manner at the right time. Once the process is rolling, it is very difficult and costly to change the objectives of a clinical trial to accommodate marketing requests. This applies to nonclinical as well as clinical outcomes evaluations and measurements.

SPEED TO MARKET VERSUS PRODUCT PROMOTION PREFERENCES

A difficult decision that may face the product development planning team: is it better to pursue a quicker path to marketing approval by limiting the testing—particularly the clinical testing—to support limited claims, or to delay market entry but be able to launch a product that has been approved for more extensive, valuable indications? The answer will depend on financial resources available to initially bring the product to market, the competitive milieu, anticipated future competition, and sales projections for limited indications compared with projections for broader indications. Bringing a product to market early to establish a market presence and identity, even with curtailed promotional opportunities, has benefits and drawbacks, but should be considered in the planning process.

INTELLECTUAL PROPERTY

Intellectual property (IP) is one of the most important assets of medical products companies. It is the foundation for market dominance and continuing profitability, and is frequently the key objective in mergers and acquisitions. Recognizing the value of an IP portfolio is critical to effective product development planning. There are four major categories of IP: copyrights, trademarks, patents, and trade secrets (see Table 16.1). Consideration of all of these is essential in technology assessment, but patents may be the most germane to product development. Patents confer exclusionary rights to the patent holder. That is, a patent permits the patentee to exclude others from

Table 16.1   Types of intellectual property (IP).

IP	Description
Patent (U.S.)	The grant of a property right to the inventor for a term of 20 years from the date of filing. A patent confers the right to exclude others from making, using, offering for sale, or selling the invention in the US.
Trademark	A word, name, symbol, or device which is used in trade with goods to indicate the source of the goods and to distinguish them from the goods of others.
Copyright	A form of protection provided to the authors of original works of authorship, both published and unpublished, giving the owner the exclusive right to reproduce or distribute copies of the original work.
Trade Secret	Information that is not generally known but that gives the owner a competitive advantage, such as patentable (but unpatented) inventions, manufacturing techniques, business methods, etc. The owner must take precautions to ensure that this form of IP remains secret, since there are no rights conferred to protect the owner from competitors who independently develop or discover the trade secret.

making, selling, or using the patented invention; a patent does not permit the patentee to do anything with the patent. IP rights are territorial. That is, rights must be sought and granted separately for various parts of the world. Something patentable in the United States may already be proprietary elsewhere, and vice versa.

There would be no pharmaceutical or medical device industries without the benefits of IP. Patents protect early-stage innovation, reducing financial risk and providing encouragement to make the required investments in R&D for innovative therapies; they provide manufacturers who have made the investment to develop a product for FDA approval the opportunity to realize commercial value through exclusivity; and they are integral in the creation of a competitive generic drug market, and its concomitant consumer advantage, following the expiration of the patent rights.

For the purpose of medical product development planning, the strength of an IP portfolio depends on a number of general factors that must be questioned and evaluated: coverage, competitiveness, marketability, territory, licensability, enforceability, and patent life (see Figure 16.1).

IP conflicts occur, with good reason, primarily over medical devices with high market potential, and over the attempt to introduce generic versions of drugs (there are no generic biologics as yet). Large companies are often willing to risk the cost of patent litigation in order to corner a market, even for a limited time. When hundreds of millions of dollars and a decade

1. *Coverage.* Does the IP position really address and protect the invention in all of its aspects, including product composition, processing steps, intermediate products, and final product?

2. *Competitiveness.* Is the IP really able to exclude competitors from designing around the patent to produce essentially the same product?

3. *Marketability.* Who are the customers that would be interested in the property, and how important is the IP likely to be to them?

4. *Territory.* In what parts of the world does the IP confer exclusivity rights—domestic only, or international?

5. *Licensability.* What is the prospect of licensing the IP to another party, and what value will this bring to the patentee?

6. *Enforceability.* Are the claims defensible, and how will the IP stand up in a court of law—whether the patentee is the challenger or is being challenged?

7. *Patent life.* What is the remaining period of exclusivity offered by the IP? Can patent coverage period be extended through legislative provisions (e.g., the Hatch-Waxman Act, which allows restoration of a portion of a patent term to help compensate for time lost during clinical testing and FDA review)?

Figure 16.1 Important factors influencing IP value in medical product development planning.

or more are invested in developing a new drug, which may have annual sales potential of a billion dollars or more, it is not surprising that the original patentee will go to great lengths to defend the IP against competitors. The term of a new patent is 20 years, but by the time that a typical new drug can be marketed, there are only about 8.5 years of effective life left before its patent runs out. Even with the partial restoration added by the Hatch-Waxman Act (which restores a portion of the patent term that is used up in the clinical and FDA review process), the effective remaining patent life is only about 11 years.[53]

Conversely, there is a financial incentive to introduce a generic version, to design around existing patents, or to take a chance at willfully infringing an existing patent to get a piece of that same market. Open a national newspaper on any given day, and you'll likely find coverage of a medical product patent dispute.

DON'T FORGET THE BUDGET

Preparation of a budget for Phase 2—*feasibility,* is challenging, to say the least. In product development, there is a tendency to overlook things like patent expenses, and to underestimate costs for clinical trials. Obviously, because of their enormous diversity, there is no universal formula that can be applied to the cost of developing a medical product.

Table 16.2 is intended to be a sobering reminder of elements that may have to appear on the budget that the product development planning team presents to the review committee. Depending on the product, there are provisions for reduced patent and user fees for small companies or for first filings. Some products, such as orphan drugs, are eligible for relief from user fees.

Table 16.2 Some budget considerations.

Item	Purpose	Potential Cost ($) FY 2004
Patent	Exclude competition	• Attorney Fees: 10,000–50,000 • Filing Fee: 770–2200+ • Issue Fee: 1330 (for U.S. Utility Patents)
Preclinical Testing	Establish sufficient safety and efficacy to proceed with clinical trials in humans	10,000–100 million+
Clinical Trials	Demonstrate safety and efficacy	2 million–80 million+
FDA User Fees*	Fund additional FDA resources to improve product review	• 510(k): 2784 • PMA: 206,811 • NDA/BLA: 573,500** Establishments: 226,800 Products: 36,080

* Certain conditions may provide eligibility for reduced fees or waivers.

** For applications requiring clinical data.

Sources: (U.S. Patent and Trademark Office Fees and FDA Fees), Federal Register (14 July 2003 and 1 August 2003)

The details and requirements are beyond the scope of this book, but each new product opportunity should be assessed for money-saving options.

WHAT ABOUT GAME THEORY?

Being on a team is easy. Maintaining team spirit is not so easy. Sometimes team members appear to play games to divert attention or resources to self-centered interests, rather than to a common goal, and dealing with management seems yet another type of game. The organization clearly does not function as a single organism.

Formally, *game theory* is a branch of mathematics that deals with social situations involving two or more players, in which the interests of the players are interconnected or interdependent. It is considered a theory of rational decision making that can be applied in social situations in which each player's outcome or fate depends on what the other players do. In game theory, the term "players" can refer to individuals or groups of any size—teams, companies, armies, governments, and so on. There has been a great deal of interest in developing game theory to be a unifying force that can be applied to all interactions between and among people. Game theory models have been tailored to economics, business, psychology, politics, and history. Some experts believe that game theory is a crucial tool for understanding the modern business world, and that it has the potential to revolutionize the way people think about business.[54]

In its simplest form, game theory entails what are called zero-sum games and non-zero-sum games, and involves issues of competition, cooperation, and value.

Zero-sum games are situations of absolute conflict. Value is neither created nor destroyed, because one player's gain is equal to the other player's loss. Zero-sum games are "win–lose" in the extreme. Patent litigation over a generic drug entry can be a zero-sum game. The element of value is market share. If the pioneer company wins, it gets to keep (at least for some period of time) the piece of the market that would have gone to the generic manufacturer, while the generic challenger loses its potential market share. Alternatively, if the generic company prevails, it wins by being allowed to compete by selling the drug, while the pioneer company loses whatever share of the market the generic company will gain.

Non-zero-sum games exist when conflict is less than total, which is the more common condition in business. Outcomes that are favorable, at least to some extent, to all players, are obtainable through reaching an acceptable balance of value sharing. This is the classic win–win scenario. No one wins everything, but everybody gets something. The extent and nature of the compromise determine the outcome, so there is no absolute equilibrium. Each player may place a different value on the prize, and experience a different degree of pain with its sacrifice.

The relevance of the basic principles of game theory to social interactions seems obvious. When competitive players cooperate, they can both gain. When they don't cooperate, it is possible either that one will win and the other lose, or that both will lose. Most game scenarios that will be encountered in the development of medical products will be non-zero-sum games involving multiple players and varying degrees of cooperation and competition.

The big problem with applying game theory tactics to strategic decisions is this: "Underlying the entire structure of game theory is the key assumption that players in a game are *rational*. As game theorists use this term, rationality simply means that a player in an interactive situation will act to bring about the most preferred of the possible outcomes, given the constraint that the other players are also acting in the same way."[55] Right away, you can see the predicament. Even if you exclude those incontestably irrational people you work with, the concept of rationality is relative. What would constitute preferred outcomes in a given situation is relative. The assumption that there is an absolute agreement on the establishment of either rationality or what constitutes preferred outcomes completely ignores human factors, and of all people, those involved in medical product development planning know that you can't do that.

Globalization has brought greater access to valuable ideas, practices, technologies, and opportunities. Yet despite the unifying accomplishments of globalization, cultural differences remain an influential determinant in international economic and business relations. Because of globalization, the determinants of rationality, value, and preferred outcomes can be quite varied. One only has to reflect on the discord that has been encountered in the establishment of the European Union to see substantial disparity in the concept of value: who should or should not be members, who did or did not want to be members, acceptance of the unified currency, resource allocation. Yet in the framework of the entire world, Europe is a rather homogeneous place.

In a cultural context, some players may be averse to debate, and therefore appear cryptic or ambivalent in discussions and negotiations. The preference of outcomes may diverge among players because of cultural differences in the importance of individualism versus collectivism. Participation, strategy, and decision-making processes may be tied to cultural predilections toward showing emotion, willingness to wait for resolution, risk aversion, even attitudes toward the other players, for example, degree of deference toward authority, hostility toward specific ethnic or cultural groups, opinions about women in business. All of these disparate behaviors and opinions can and do, of course, exist also among individuals in what could be considered culturally homogeneous groups. Globalization has simply provided the opportunity for more visibility and greater exposure to such diversity. There exists a need to be sensitive to different viewpoints while maintaining the focus and goals of the team.

By the way, anticipate that situational conflict will also exist at some level and to some degree between the product development planning team and the FDA. Conflict, cooperation, and compromise with the people who make and enforce the rules of the game present a unique set of issues that affect rationality and the mutuality of preferred outcomes.

These concerns are not intended to scoff at game theory, but rather to caution against personalization of the determinants. It is as important to understand your friend as it is to understand your foe. But in our shrinking and often chaotic world, it's becoming more difficult to imagine switching places with any other player in the game.

QUALITY CHALLENGES

At the soul of TQM lies the refusal to accept business as usual. The application of quality principles to all company endeavors—including new product development—strives to make tomorrow's activities more effective and productive than today's. Product development planning should be thought of as applying TQM principles to new healthcare products.

There are some aspects of TQM that make its application to medical product development organizations more challenging than its application to other areas, such as manufacturing. In fact, research groups and development groups are among the most notoriously resistant to quality management programs. Ask anyone who is both basically knowledgeable of TQM and intimately involved in product development, especially any scientist, and reasons why TQM can't work in product development will easily spring to his or her mind. This rationalization is usually based on the following arguments.

The Incremental Focus of TQM Is Incompatible with the Saltatory Nature of Scientific Discoveries and Advances. It is generally accepted that scientific change is not the steady, incremental acquisition of knowledge. Rather, it is characterized by relatively static periods during which progress revolves around solving problems within the context of what is known and accepted as dogma, punctuated by explosive revolutions that completely change the way we view the world. Therefore, it makes no sense to force-fit inventive technical efforts into a paradigm of incremental improvement.

Monitoring Tactics and Measurement Systems Stifle Creativity. In product development, adherence to certain processes (such as test protocols and documentation requirements) is mandatory, but there may be resistance to process overload when the driving factor seems to be philosophic or social rather than scientific or regulatory. Creative individuals often bridle and dig in their heels when they are told that they must oblige yet another set of requirements involving process, charts, checklists, and measurements. This leads to locking horns with those individuals who are inflexibly driven, perhaps controlled, by process, charts, checklists, and measurements.

Speaking of Measurements, There Are Obvious Difficulties Associated with Applying Quality Metrics to Creative Endeavors. Quality measurements typically associated with TQM are—because they are originally manufacturing-based—difficult to apply to product development. For example, a defect rate per million units manufactured cannot be translated into product development efforts. On the other side of the coin, technical people who are used to precision indices, such as pH or tensile strength, are also often uncomfortable with soft subjective qualitative TQM metrics, such as customer satisfaction.

Management Requires Buy-in and Adherence to TQM Principles but Does Not Support Those Involved in Product Development in a Manner that Allows Them to Succeed at TQM. In some companies, product development scientists are deliberately isolated from customers; other scientists are disinterested in customers and market issues. Meanwhile, marketing associates are often unwilling to understand or assimilate any technical information; regulatory affairs professionals can regard themselves as members of a secret society with knowledge and information that is shared reluctantly; and manufacturing people may not want to be bothered until they have a defined product to make. Few, if any, of the product development team members have been prepared to grasp the big picture of customer requirements, market need, competitive environment, technical limitations, quality issues, manufacturability, or regulatory constraints.

Acknowledging these issues as obstacles to TQM fundamentally negates the underlying principle of not being satisfied with business as usual. It implies a rigidity in the practice of TQM that is, in itself, incompatible with the TQM philosophy. Implying that TQM comprises specific defined programs and metrics systems that must be applied to all aspects of a business is fallacious, and this attitude does not befit quality management.

Therefore, it is likely to be necessary to effect a cultural change to integrate an understanding of quality processes in healthcare product development organizations. Quality procedures and standards that apply to significant but specific healthcare product development planning activities have already been discussed. They include:

- GLPs

- GCPs

- Design controls

Viewing product development planning as a TQM program, which includes the quality practices inherent in GLPs, GCPs, and—in the case of medical devices—design controls, will facilitate acceptance of a TQM philosophy and recognition of the applicability of TQM to product development.

It is important to always remember that quality is all about customer satisfaction and that the concept of quality encompasses the finished product and all supporting services. The healthcare product development process component of product development planning includes such important post-launch support.

Quality can be defined as conformance to agreed-upon customer requirements. Customers may be external customers, such as the end users of a product, or internal customers. To attain quality a product development organization must therefore know both its internal and external customers, understand its customers' needs, and share a commitment to satisfying customer needs. One must think in terms of an infinite continuum; quality is what the customer wants, and what the customer wants is quality (see Figure 16.2). How a product development organization can achieve its quality management goals will depend a great deal on the nature of the products being developed and the corporate environment in which the organization must work. For example, a good place for a medical device product development organization to kick off its quality management process initiative would be through attention to elements of design controls. Focus on the

Figure 16.2   The customer/quality continuum.

customer via human factors analyses and customer needs assessment will simultaneously fulfill an FDA requirement, shorten development time, and define the expectations of the end-use customer. Failure mode analyses will allow anticipation of potential design deficiencies so that the final product design will satisfy the customer.

There is a compelling need to divorce the product development organization from the notion that quality is something attained through the process of inspection and the removal of defective product. Rather than assuming that problems can be fixed ex post facto, those involved in health-care product development must be committed to preventing problems. There are no universal, standardized methods or solutions for achieving quality. Every product development organization must find its own way, regularly reevaluating quality strategies with an eye set on customer satisfaction and continuous improvement.

17

Where Do We Go from Here?

When you come to a fork in the road, take it.

—Yogi Berra

In the long run, you hit what you aim at, so aim high.

—Henry David Thoreau

Witty people have summarized the new product development process in six phases.[56] Sadly, what makes these words humorous is the truth that we recognize in them. The purpose of product development planning is to ensure that the development of new healthcare products does not follow this course.

Phase 1: Euphoria. Everything looks good—the market potential is enormous and the profits unlimited. Management sees all of the positives. The project is a definite "go."

Phase 2: Disenchantment. A few glitches are identified; problems begin to occur. The market might not be quite as big as first thought, and there could be a few issues with safety, efficacy, or manufacturability. The project is a bit more complex than was originally thought. Management does not like disenchantment, so it adheres to its stand on euphoria.

Phase 3: Chaos. Everyone tries to support management, because everyone knows what happens to negative people and to bearers of bad news. Frantic efforts are made to keep things looking good in the face of contrary evidence. Management is convinced that an incompetent product development team is the reason that euphoria is slipping away. Outside experts and consultants are brought in to analyze and correct the situation.

Phase 4: Search for the guilty. Someone obviously has to be blamed for the problem, but the mess is complex. Who is responsible?

Phase 5: Punishment of the innocent. The selection is made of those who will fall upon the sword. There is no one to defend those who are sacrificed.

Phase 6: Promotion of the uninvolved. Nonparticipants are rewarded. They must have had considerable insight and intelligence to stay away from the project in the first place.

IN CLOSING

There are a number of points that should be made but that do not fit neatly into any of the preceding chapters. There are also a number of points that have already been made, but that warrant additional emphasis. So the closing paragraphs of this book offer some exhortations and admonitions.

As members of product development teams interact, there is sometimes conflict caused by traditional and dogmatic views of the relative importance of the models of innovation known as *market pull* and *technology push.* Market pull ideas are those generated by the marketplace because of unmet customer needs; the search is for technology solutions to meet the identified needs. Technology push ideas are generated from the drive to exploit an existing technology by finding additional uses for it; the search is for market needs that can be met by the technology platform. Turf battles between marketing and technical team members over which function takes precedence can impede idea generation and evaluation.

In medical product development, market pull and technology push models should not exist independently. Most healthcare companies have invested a great deal of time and money in their technologies, and the incentive and economy of applying these technology bases to addressing new or expanded market needs is understandably strong. Conversely, when an important unmet market need exists, the search for and development of new technologies that might prove effective will be of vital importance. Yet acquiring that new effective technology in itself will drive the push to find additional market applications for it. In a medical product development organization, the innovative process involves linking both courses, so that viable options are never overlooked. A flexible and creative company can simultaneously build on its core technologies and respond to both changing market and technological needs. A strategic fusion of market pull and technology push is the answer.

Maintaining medical product development momentum in an era of moving regulatory targets and of vague and vacillating political and economic pressures is difficult. Add to this the difficulties resulting from organizational rearrangements and redefinitions, and it's a wonder that new products are developed at all. Disruptive environmental factors are stressful and counterproductive to development efforts. Defining and adhering to practices consistent with those encompassed in product development planning will facilitate continuity and progress throughout management changes and presidential administrations.

Product development is a path that turns an idea into something that is useful and valuable to customers and that is profitable for the company. Embracing the principles of product development planning will make the journey down the path to new medical products safer, faster, and more enjoyable.

A few closing thoughts before we end:

- Think in terms of looking for solutions, not just for products.

- Haste is not equivalent to speed.

- Don't become a slave to process. Processes should be tools, not drivers.

- Act on the plans that result from the exercises involved in product development planning. If you're just going to put them into a binder for distribution and then forget about them, everyone's time will have been wasted.

- Listen to the voice of the customer.

- Put quality above all else.

- View product development planning as applying TQM principles to new product development.

- Go forth and develop new medical products!

Endnotes

1. National Center for Health Statistics, *Health, United States, 2002* (Hyattsville, MD: Public Health Service, 2002).
2. Centers for Medicare and Medicaid Services, Office of the Actuary, *National Health Expenditures 2001 Version* (January 2003).
3. John F. Schaefer, "Recent Advances in Medical Technology," *Regulatory Affairs Focus* 8 (January 2001): 8–11.
4. John T. Kelly, "The Drug Development and Approval Process," in *New Drug Approvals in 2002* (Washington, DC: Pharmaceutical Research and Manufacturers of America, 2003): 17.
5. See note 3.
6. Food and Drug Administration Modernization Act of 1997, PL 105 (1997).
7. U.S. Department of Health and Human Services, Public Health Service, Food and Drug Administration, *Requirements of Laws and Regulations Enforced by the U.S. Food and Drug Administration,* DHHS Publication no. 89-1115 (1989).
8. *Federal Food, Drug, and Cosmetic Act,* U.S. Code, vol. 21, secs. 301–92.
9. *Public Health Service Act,* U.S. Code, vol. 42, secs. 262–63.
10. Jonathan S. Kahan, "FDA Regulatory Programs: Cooperation and Common Sense Typify a Record of Success," *Medical Device and Diagnostic Industry* 18, no. 5 (1996): 88–99.
11. *Federal Food, Drug, and Cosmetic Act,* U.S. Code, vol. 21, secs. 301–92.
12. *Medtronic, Inc. v. Lohr,* 116 Sup. Ct. 2240 (1996).
13. "Medical Devices; Preemption of State Product Liability Claims," *Federal Register* 62, no. 239 (12 December 1997): 65384–88.
14. Restatement (Third) of Torts: Product Liability 2 (1998).

15. U.S. Department of Health and Human Services, Public Health Service, Food and Drug Administration, Center for Drug Evaluation and Review, *CDER Handbook.*

16. John T. Kelly, "The Drug Development and Approval Process," *New Drug Approvals in 2002* (January 2003): 17.

17. Prescription Drug User Fee Act of 1992.

18. John T. Kelly, "The Drug Development and Approval Process," *New Drug Approvals in 2002* (January 2003): 17.

19. John F. Schaefer, "Recent Advances in Medical Technology," *Regulatory Affairs Focus* 8 (January 2003): 8–11.

20. "Medical Devices: Exemption from Pemarked Notification and Reserved Devices; Class I," *Federal Register* 63, no. 21 (2 February 1998): 5387–93.

21. U.S. Department of Health and Human Services, Public Health Service, Food and Drug Administration, Center for Devices and Radiological Health, *Office of Device Evaluation Annual Report, Fiscal Year 2002.*

22. *Medtronic, Inc. v. Lohr,* 116 Sup. Ct. 2240 (1996).

23. U.S. Department of Health and Human Services, Food and Drug Administration, Center for Devices and Radiological Health, "Design Controls," *Quality System Manual.*

24. Procedures for Performing Failure Mode, Effects, and Criticality Analysis, Military Standards MIL-STD-1629A (24 November 1980).

25. U.S. Food and Drug Administration, "Managing the Risks from Medical Product Use: Creating a Risk Management Framework" (May 1999).

26. Lou Morris, Judy Jones, Suellen Curkendall, and Judith Sills, "The New Era of Risk Management," *Pharmaceutical Executive* (July 2002): 50–58.

27. Peter L. Knepell, "Integrating Risk Management with Design Control," *Device & Diagnostic Industry* (October 1998).

28. U.S. Food and Drug Administration, Center for Devices and Radiological Health, "Preproduction Quality Assurance Planning: Recommendations for Medical Device Manufacturers," *CDRH Manual* (27 March 1997).

29. Procedures for Performing Failure Mode, Effects, and Criticality Analysis, Military Standards MIL-STD-1629A (24 November 1980).

30. U.S. Food and Drug Administration, "Protecting the Public Health: FDA Pursues Aggressive Enforcement Strategy," white paper (30 June 2003).

31. U.S. Department of Health and Human Services, Food and Drug Administration, Office of Regulatory Affairs, *Regulatory Procedures Manual* (August 1997).

32. Karen E. Lasser, Paul D. Allen, Steffie J. Woolhandler, David U. Himmelstein, Sidney M. Wolfe, and David H. Bor, "Timing of New Black Box Warnings and Withdrawals for Prescription Medications," *JAMA* 287 (2002): 2215–20.

33. U.S. Department of Health and Human Services, Food and Drug Administration, Center for Drug Evaluation and Research, "Drug Safety and Quality," *CDER Report to the Nation: 2001* (May 2002).

34. James G. Dickinson, "FDA and the Device Industry: A Tale of Suspicion," *Medical Device & Diagnostic Industry* (May 1996).

35. Dick Sawyer and CDRH Work Group, "Do It by Design: An Introduction to Human Factors in Medical Devices" (December 1996).

36. Michael E. Wiklund, "Human Factors Guidelines," *Medical Device & Diagnostic Industry* 17, no. 12 (1995): 28–32.

37. Linda T. Kohn, Janet M. Corrigan, and Molly S. Donaldson, eds., *To Err Is Human: Building a Safer Health System* (Washington, DC: National Academy Press, November 1999).

38. Dorothy Leonard-Barton, *Wellsprings of Knowledge* (Boston: Harvard Business School Press, 1995).

39. "New Drug and Biological Drug Products; Evidence Needed to Demonstrate Effectiveness of New Drugs When Human Efficacy Studies Are Not Ethical or Feasible," *Federal Register* 67, no. 105 (31 May 2002).

40. John T. Kelly, "The Drug Development and Approval Process," *New Drug Approvals in 2002* (Pharmaceuticals Research and Manufacturing Association, January 2003).

41. U.S. Department of Health and Human Services, Food and Drug Administration, *Good Laboratory Practice for Nonclinical Laboratory Studies,* 21 CFR ch. 1, part 58 (1 April 1995).

42. U.S. Department of Health and Human Services, Food and Drug Administration, Office of Device Evaluation, Use of International Standard ISO 10993, "Biological Evaluation of Medical Devices Part 1: Evaluation and Testing," general program memorandum G95-1 (May 1995).

43. International Conference on Harmonization, "Draft Guideline on Good Clinical Practice," *Federal Register* 60, no. 159 (17 August 1995): 42948–42957.

44. "Statistics on Drug Development: Cost/Complexity, Development Time, Success Rates," in *Pharmaceutical R&D Sourcebook 2000* (Boston: Paraxel International Corp., 2000).

45. International Conference on Harmonisation; "Draft Guidance on M4 Common Technical Document; Availability," *Federal Register* 65, no. 165 (24 August 2000): 51621–24.

46. U.S. Department of Health and Human Services, Food and Drug Administration, "Guidance for Industry: Collection of Race and Ethnicity Data in Clinical Trials (draft)" (January 2003).

47. Mark Zitter, "Outcomes Assessment: True Customer Focus Comes to Healthcare," *Medical Interface* (May 1992): 32–37.

48. Joyce A. Cramer and Bert Spilker, *Quality of Life and Pharmacoeconomics, An Introduction* (Philadelphia: Lippincott-Raven, 1998).

49. Charles J. Nuese, *Building the Right Things Right* (New York: Quality Resources, 1995).

50. Steven C. Wheelwright and Kirn B. Clark, *Revolutionizing Product Development* (New York: The Free Press, 1992).

51. Food and Drug Administration, Center for Drug Evaluation and Research, *FDA Approves First Antibiotic Treatment for Ulcers* (19 April 1996).

52. Kenneth J. Kelley, "Using Host Defenses to Fight Infectious Diseases," *Nature Biotechnology* 14, no. 5 (1996): 587–90.

53. "Delivering the Promise of Pharmaceutical Innovation: The Need to Maintain Strong and Predictable Intellectual Property Rights," white paper (Washington, DC: Pharmaceutical Research and Manufacturers of America, 22 April 2002).

54. Frank C. Zagare, *Game Theory, Concepts and Applications* (Newbury Park: Sage Publications, 1984): 8.

55. Ibid, p. 7.

56. Warren R. Stumpe, "What the Research Manager Should Know About New Product Psychology," *Research Management* 22 (1979): 13–17.

Glossary

abbreviated new drug application (ANDA)—An application for approval of a generic drug.

biologic—A biological product; a preparation made from living organisms and their products applicable to the prevention, treatment, or cure of diseases or injuries; the category of biologics includes vaccines, blood products, certain diagnostic products, and biotechnology-derived products.

biologics license application (BLA)—An application for approval of a new biological product.

clinical trials—The evaluation of a product in studies involving human subjects.

combination products—Complex medical products, such as drug-device, drug-biologic, and device-biologic combinations.

common technical document (CTD)—An international harmonized format for submissions for approval of pharmaceuticals for human use. The CTD does not replace the BLA or NDA, but provides a standardization of the presentation of content.

design controls—A system to ensure that a new medical device can be used safely and effectively while meeting customer needs; a requirement of current GMPs for medical devices.

development portfolio—The collection of projects available to or being developed by a company.

development portfolio management—One of the four integral components of product development planning; a way to maximize control and minimize risks by keeping a company's strategy for new products compatible with its business objectives.

device—See *medical device.*

drug—An article intended for use in the diagnosis, cure, mitigation, treatment, or prevention of disease, and which is intended to affect the structure or function of the body.

failure mode analysis—A determination of malfunction symptoms that appear immediately before or immediately after a failure of a critical parameter in a system or product.

Federal Food, Drug, and Cosmetic (FD&C) Act—The basic law in the United States governing foods, drugs for animals and humans, cosmetics, and medical devices. With its numerous amendments, it is the most extensive law of its kind in the world; also referred to as "the Act."

Food and Drug Administration Modernization Act—The federal act making numerous changes to the rules governing the FDA and industries regulated by the FDA.

generic drugs—Approved drugs that are no longer protected by patents and are approved for marketing by companies without the need for clinical trials; generic drugs are bioequivalent to the original approved drugs.

good clinical practice (GCP)—Regulations and policies governing clinical research.

good manufacturing practice (GMP)—Regulations that establish the minimum requirements for the methods, facilities, and controls used in the manufacturing of medical products.

human factors—The discipline that seeks to analyze and optimize the relationship between human beings and any technology; the interfaces may be physical, perceptual, or cognitive.

intellectual property—Intellectual assets, including patents, copyrights, trademarks, and trade secrets.

investigational device exemption (IDE)—An exemption to the rules prohibiting a medical device that has not been cleared or approved for marketing from being shipped and tested in human subjects.

investigational new drug (IND)—An application for permission to test an unapproved drug or biologic in human subjects. IND provides exemption to rules prohibiting the shipment of unapproved drugs.

managed care—Healthcare provided by a prepaid health plan or covered by an insurance program, in which medical services are reviewed and coordinated to manage access to care, quality of care, and cost of care.

medical device—An article intended for use in the diagnosis, cure, mitigation, treatment, or prevention of disease or other condition which does not depend on chemical action within or on the body and is not dependent upon being metabolized to achieve its primary intended purpose.

medical products—Drugs, biologics, and medical devices; these products are regulated by the FDA.

new chemical entity (NCE)—An active drug substance that has never been previously approved by the FDA. Also called *new molecular entity*.

new drug application (NDA)—An application to the FDA for approval to market a new drug.

new molecular entity (NME)—See *new chemical entity*.

outcomes research—Studies to determine whether use of a technology increases survival, reduces morbidity, improves quality of life, and provides benefits that justify the cost of its use.

pharmacoeconomics—The application of economic principles to the evaluation of pharmaceutical interventions.

portfolio—See development portfolio.

preclinical studies—Evaluations of safety and/or efficacy in *in vitro, ex vivo*, or *in vivo* systems other than in human beings.

premarket approval (PMA) application—An application made to the FDA for approval to market certain types of medical devices (Class III) that are considered life-supporting, life-sustaining, or of substantial importance in preventing impairment of human health.

premarket notification application [510(k)]—A submission made to the FDA to gain clearance for commercial distribution and marketing of certain types of medical devices (Class II and some Class I); clearance may be gained by a finding that the device is substantially equivalent to another Class II or Class I device that is already on the market in the United States.

product development planning—An integrative approach to addressing both long-term and short-term needs and requirements for new products. The four main components are product development process, development portfolio management, technology assessment, and technology forecasting.

product development process—One of the four integral components of product development planning; it describes the stages of healthcare product development (discovery, feasibility, optimization, demonstration, production, and launch and follow-through), as well as the associated tasks, reviews, and deliverables for each stage.

Public Health Service (PHS) Act—A federal act covering a broad spectrum of health concerns, including the regulation of biological products for human use.

quality—What the customer wants; the characteristic of a product or service that meets customer expectations and is free from defects.

quality system regulations (QSR)—Medical device GMPs.

recall—The removal or correction, by a firm, of a marketed product because the product is considered to be in violation of laws administered by FDA.

risk assessment—The process of identifying, estimating, and evaluating the nature and severity of risks associated with a product; also called *risk analysis* or *hazard analysis.*

technology assessment—One of the four integral components of product development planning; it is an ongoing identification and evaluation of existing, new, emerging, and embryonic technologies.

technology forecasting—One of the four integral components of product development planning; anticipating the future to allow the formation of a suitable and planned technology strategy.

total quality management (TQM)—The application of quality principles to all company endeavors, with an emphasis on customer satisfaction and continuous improvement.

user fees—Fees paid to the FDA by manufacturers for the review of applications for clearance or approval of new drugs, biologics, and medical devices. The fees provide additional funds to the FDA to improve the product review process.

Resources

ORGANIZATIONS

AAMI (Association for the Advancement of Medical Instrumentation)
1110 North Glebe Road, Suite 220
Arlington, VA 22201-4595
703-525-4890
Fax: 703-276-0793
www.aami.org

AAMI is an alliance of engineering, medicine, nursing, industry, and government professionals with a mission to assist in the development, evaluation, acquisition, use, and maintenance of medical devices and instrumentation.

ACRP (Association of Clinical Research Professionals)
500 Montgomery Street, Suite 800
Alexandria, VA 22314
703-254-8100
Fax: 703-254-8101
www.acrpnet.org

ACRP is the primary resource for clinical research professionals in the pharmaceutical, biotechnology, and medical device industries, as well as those in hospitals, academic medical centers, and physician office settings.

AdvaMed (Advanced Medical Technology Association;
  formerly HIMA)
1200 G Street NW, Suite 400
Washington, DC 20005-3814
202-783-8700
Fax: 202-783-8750
www.advamed.org

AdvaMed is the largest medical technology association in the world, representing more than 1100 innovators and manufacturers of medical devices, diagnostic products, and medical information systems.

ASQ (American Society for Quality)
600 North Plankinton Avenue
Milwaukee, WI 53203
800-248-1946 or 414-272-8575
Fax: 414-272-1734
www.asq.org

ASQ is a source for information on the development, promotion, and application of quality strategies and techniques. ASQ makes its officers and member experts available to inform and advise the U.S. Congress, government agencies, state legislatures, and other groups and individuals on quality-related topics.

BIO (Biotechnology Industry Organization)
1225 Eye Street, NW, Suite 400
Washington, DC 20005
202-962-9200
www.bio.org

BIO is an umbrella organization uniting biotechnology organizations; BIO serves as an advocate of the industry's positions to elected officials and regulators, to inform media about the industry's progress, and to provide business development services to its member companies.

FDLI (Food and Drug Law Institute)
1000 Vermont Ave. NW, Suite 200
Washington, DC 20005
800-956-6293 or 202-371-1420
Fax: 202-371-0649
www.fdli.org

FDLI is the leading impartial forum for the FDA, other government agencies, and the legal, business, academic and consumer communities to engage in the exchange of information and perspectives on issues relating to products regulated by the FDA.

GPhA (Generic Pharmaceutical Association)
2300 Clarendon Blvd., Suite 400
Arlington, VA 22201
703-647-2480
Fax: 703-647-2481
www.gphaonline.org

GPhA provides information to consumers and manufacturers on issues facing the generics industry.

ICH (International Conference on Harmonization of Technical Requirements for Registration of Pharamceuticals for Human Use)
ICH Secretariat
c/o IFPMA
30 rue de St-Jean, PO Box 758
1211 Geneva 13, Switzerland
+41 22 338 32 06
Fax: +41 22 338 32 30
www.ich.org

ICH is a unique project that brings together the regulatory authorities of Europe, Japan, and the United States with experts from the pharmaceutical industry in these three regions to discuss scientific and technical aspects of product registration.

ISPE (International Society for Pharmaceutical Engineering)
3109 W. Dr. Martin Luther King, Jr. Blvd., Suite 250
Tampa, FL 33607
813-960-2105
Fax: 813-264-2816
www.ispe.org

ISPE promotes the advancement and interests of engineers and other technical professionals in the healthcare manufacturing industry.

LES (Licensing Executives Society)
1800 Diagonal Road, Suite 280
Alexandria, VA 22314
703-836-3106
Fax: 703-836-3107
www.LES.org

LES is an international professional society whose members are involved in the transfer, use, development, manufacture, and marketing of intellectual property.

MDMA (Medical Device Manufacturers Association)
1900 K Street, NW, Suite 300
Washington, DC 20006
202-496-7150
Fax: 202-496-7756
www.medicaldevices.org

MDMA is a national trade association representing independent manufacturers of medical devices, diagnostic products, and healthcare information systems.

PDA (Parenteral Drug Association)
3 Bethesda Metro Center, Suite 1500
Bethesda, MD 20814
301-656-5900
Fax: 301-986-0296
www.pda.org

PDA is an international educational organization of more than 10,500 individual members involved in the manufacture, development, and research of pharmaceuticals and related products.

PhRMA (Pharmaceutical Research and Manufacturers of America)
1100 Fifteenth Street, NW
Washington, DC 20005
202-835-3400
Fax: 202-835-3414
www.phrma.org

PhRMA represents the country's leading research-based pharmaceutical and biotechnology companies.

PQRI (Product Quality Researach Institute)
2107 Wilson Blvd., Suite 700
Arlington, VA 22201-3042
703-247-4719
Fax: 703-525-7136
www.PQRI.org

PQRI is a collaboration involving FDA-CDER, industry, and academia, whose initiative is to help identify the types of product quality information that should be submitted in regulatory filings to CDER.

RAPS (Regulatory Affairs Professionals Society)
11300 Rockville Pike, Suite 1000
Rockville, MD 20852
301-770-2920
Fax: 301-770-2924
www.raps.org

RAPS is the foremost international professional society representing the healthcare regulatory affairs profession. RAPS represents individuals, government workers, corporations, academia, and research and nonprofit organizations.

GOVERNMENT HEALTH STATISTICS

Agency for Healthcare Research and Quality (AHRQ)
www.ahcpr.gov

AHRQ provides evidence-based information on healthcare outcomes; quality; and cost, use, and access.

National Center for Health Statistics (NCHS)
www.cdc.gov/nchs

NCHS provides compilations of U.S. statistical information to guide actions and policies to improve the health of the people.

Centers for Medicare & Medicaid Services (CMS, formerly HCFA)
www.cms.hhs.gov/researchers/statsdata.asp

The Centers for Medicare & Medicaid Services specializes in statistics, data, and research information. CMS offers a broad range of quantitative information to researchers and other healthcare professionals.

REGULATIONS

Code of Federal Regulations (CFR)
www.access.gpo.gov/nara/cfr

Federal Register (FR)
www.gpoaccess.gov/fr/index.html

Food and Drug Administration Modernization Act (FDAMA)
www.fda.gov/cder/guidance/105-115.htm
www.fda.gov/cdrh/modact97.pdf

Food Drug & Cosmetic Act (FD&C)
www.fda.gov/opacom/laws/fdcact/fdctoc.htm

Public Health Service Act (PHS)
www.fda.gov/opacom/laws/phsvcact/phsvcact.htm

FOOD AND DRUG ADMINISTRATION

Food and Drug Administration (FDA)
5600 Fishers Lane
Rockville, MD 20857
888-463-6332
Main Web site: www.fda.gov
Alphabetical Web site index: www.fda.gov/opacom/hpchoice.html
Index of contact information: www.fda.gov/comments.html

Center for Biologics Evaluation and Research (CBER)
www.fda.gov/cber

Center for Drug Evaluation and Research (CDER)
www.fda.gov/cder

Center for Devices and Radiological Health (CDRH)
www.fda.gov/cdrh

Office of Combination Products (OCP)
www.fda.gov/oc/combination

INDUSTRY SUPPORT

CBER: Manufacturers Assistance Page
www.fda.gov/cber/manufacturer.htm

CDER: Small Business Assistance
www.fda.gov/cder/about/smallbiz

CDRH: Division of Small Manufacturers, International, and Consumer Assistance (DSMICA)/Device Advice
www.fda.gov/cdrh/industry/support

Index